Heroku Cookbook

Over 70 step-by-step recipes to solve the challenges of administering and scaling a real-world production web application on Heroku

Mike Coutermarsh

[PACKT]
PUBLISHING

BIRMINGHAM - MUMBAI

Heroku Cookbook

First published: November 2014

Production reference: 1181114

Published by Packt Publishing Ltd.
Livery Place
35 Livery Street
Birmingham B3 2PB, UK.

ISBN 978-1-78217-794-4

www.packtpub.com

Cover image by Pratyush Mohanta (tysoncinematics@gmail.com)

Credits

Author
Mike Coutermarsh

Reviewers
Jon Ferry

Mads Ohm Larsen

Mwaki Harri Magotswi

Peter Robinett

Kien Nguyen Trung

Commissioning Editor
Grant Mizen

Acquisition Editor
Greg Wild

Content Development Editor
Arvind Koul

Technical Editor
Shruti Rawool

Copy Editors
Karuna Narayanan

Laxmi Subramanian

Project Coordinator
Neha Bhatnagar

Proofreaders
Simran Bhogal

Maria Gould

Ameesha Green

Paul Hindle

Indexer
Monica Ajmera Mehta

Production Coordinator
Alwin Roy

Cover Work
Alwin Roy

About the Author

Mike Coutermarsh has been building and deploying web applications for over 10 years. Originally from New Hampshire, he now works and lives in Boston, MA. As an early adopter of Heroku, he's been working with and writing about the technology for over 5 years. He works as a software engineer for Product Hunt (http://www.producthunt.com). Previously, he's built and scaled web applications at Gazelle (https://www.gazelle.com/) and was a cofounder of Taskk. When Mike isn't coding or writing, you will usually find him making the perfect cup of coffee, watching hockey, or at the gym.

This book would not exist if it were not for the incredible support of my family, friends, and coworkers. I would like to thank my family, mom, dad, Ben, Kayleigh, and Tucker, who were always so encouraging and supportive. To my friends who were always so understanding when I "had to write", thank you. Thank you Greg and Arvind at Packt Publishing for being so helpful and patient; I've grown so much as a writer because of your guidance. To my technical reviewers, you are the best; thank you for your many hours of reviewing the drafts and invaluable feedback. Finally, I would like to thank the reader for joining me; I hope you learn to love deploying code as much as I do.

About the Reviewers

Jon Ferry has been designing and developing web-based software in a variety of technologies for over 14 years. He has 5 years of experience developing production-level Ruby applications on Heroku's stack. A graduate from the Rochester Institute of Technology, he currently works as a technical lead at Dealer.com.

For more information about Jon and his projects, visit `http://jonferry.com` or follow him on Twitter at `@jonferry`.

Mads Ohm Larsen is a full-stack Ruby on Rails developer, gradually shifting to DevOps. He has, in his line of work, deployed and optimized multiple Rails, Sinatra, and Grape apps on Heroku, using multiple Rubies, including JRuby for better performance. His recent switch to DevOps has allowed him even more insight into the world of optimization.

Mwaki Harri Magotswi, raised in Nairobi, Kenya, started tinkering with computer hardware at the age of 16. This interest led him to learn computer science, and later web development, where he discovered Ruby on Rails, a framework he enjoys developing on. Most recently, he was a software engineer for a recommerce firm, Gazelle, before taking a break to continue his studies. Constantly experimenting, he is currently playing with various Ruby-based blogging platforms and JavaScript MVC frameworks when time allows.

In his free time, he enjoys reading, watching TV, playing video games, watching sports, casual bike rides, scenic drives, cars, craft beers, and the occasional 15 minutes of rugby. He is also a casual traveler, food sampler, and amateur mixologist, willing to try most things at least once.

> I dedicate my work on this book to my dear late friend Sophie as well as all my family and friends who have helped me get this far.

Peter Robinett is a backend and mobile developer, with a focus on Scala and iOS development. He is a frequent user of the Heroku platform and a fan of its power and extensibility.

He is currently a developer at Lua Technologies. He also works at Bubble Foundry and blogs occasionally at www.bubblefoundry.com.

Kien Nguyen Trung is a software developer who lives in Hanoi, Vietnam. After spending years in high school learning Mathematics and achieving many rewards, he decided to challenge himself in computer science. He started learning programming from 2006 and fell in love with it.

In his free time, he builds some funny things from scratch, such as Pinterest bots to interact with Pinterest API, a Facemash clone using the Facebook avatar with face recognition, and so on. He runs a blog at http://kiennt.com to write about what he learned and his thoughts on software engineering. He spends a lot of time writing code that not only runs but is also clean and clear. His favorite quote is *Any fool can write code that a computer can understand. Good programmers write code that humans can understand* by Martin Fowler.

Since August 2012, he has been leading backend development at SimplePrints (http://getsimpleprints.com), a fast-growing start-up of 500 start-up companies. He refactors most of the backend source code in SimplePrints applications so that it is more readable and maintainable. Since June 2014, he has been designing architecture for both backend and iOS applications of SimplePrints. His favorite programming language is Python, but he also works on Ruby, JavaScript, and Objective-C.

www.PacktPub.com

Support files, eBooks, discount offers, and more

For support files and downloads related to your book, please visit www.PacktPub.com.

Did you know that Packt offers eBook versions of every book published, with PDF and ePub files available? You can upgrade to the eBook version at www.PacktPub.com and as a print book customer, you are entitled to a discount on the eBook copy. Get in touch with us at service@packtpub.com for more details.

At www.PacktPub.com, you can also read a collection of free technical articles, sign up for a range of free newsletters and receive exclusive discounts and offers on Packt books and eBooks.

https://www2.packtpub.com/books/subscription/packtlib

Do you need instant solutions to your IT questions? PacktLib is Packt's online digital book library. Here, you can search, access, and read Packt's entire library of books.

Why subscribe?

- ▸ Fully searchable across every book published by Packt
- ▸ Copy and paste, print, and bookmark content
- ▸ On demand and accessible via a web browser

Free access for Packt account holders

If you have an account with Packt at www.PacktPub.com, you can use this to access PacktLib today and view 9 entirely free books. Simply use your login credentials for immediate access.

Table of Contents

Preface

As developers, we want to spend our time focusing on building our applications. We're not interested in setting up load balancers or endlessly tweaking firewalls. We just want to easily deploy and scale our code.

Heroku has made this possible by automating and hiding the dirty details of application deployment. This has resulted in a giant leap in developer productivity, making it easier to deploy code than it was earlier.

Even though Heroku has dramatically simplified the entire process, there is still a lot that we need to know before we launch a production-level application on Heroku.

The goal of this book is to teach developers how to use Heroku effectively. You'll learn exactly what it takes to deploy and support a production-level application on Heroku. Along the way, we will learn how Heroku works behind the scenes. The more we understand, the better we will be equipped to take decisions on how our applications should be designed and written.

What this book covers

Chapter 1, *Getting Started with Heroku*, will teach you how to set up all the tools we need to get our applications ready and deployed to Heroku.

Chapter 2, *Managing Heroku from the Command Line*, informs us that Heroku's CLI is the backbone of all our interactions with our Heroku application. Here, we'll get comfortable with administering our apps from the CLI.

Chapter 3, *Setting Up a Staging Environment*, specifies how to set up a staging environment for our Heroku applications. We need a place to test our application before deploying it to production.

Chapter 4, *Production-ready with Heroku*, covers the steps needed to get a Heroku application ready to handle production-level traffic.

Chapter 5, Error Monitoring and Logging Tools, specifies how to set up logging and alerts to keep us informed about any problems with our application. We can never have too much information about our application's usage and performance.

Chapter 6, Load Testing a Heroku Application, specifies how to simulate massive spikes of traffic and get insight into our application's performance bottlenecks. The first step to improving our application's performance is being able to measure it.

Chapter 7, Optimizing Ruby Server Performance on Heroku, specifies how to choose and configure our Ruby web server for maximum performance on a Heroku dyno.

Chapter 8, Optimizing a Rails Application on Heroku, tells us how to introduce caching and reduce load times throughout our Rails applications.

Chapter 9, Using and Administrating Heroku Postgres, specifies how to pick the right plan, administer it from the CLI, and keep it healthy with various Postgres health checks, as our database is the most critical piece of our application.

Chapter 10, The Heroku Platform API, specifies how to create, scale, and manage our applications, all through the API, thus preparing us to write our own programs to interact with Heroku for us.

What you need for this book

To complete the recipes in this book, you'll need an OS X and a Linux or Windows machine. Specific setup and installation instructions for all software and applications that are needed are detailed step by step in each chapter.

Who this book is for

This book is intended for developers who want to learn what it takes to deploy and manage production-level applications on Heroku. You might have already deployed applications to Heroku or might be entirely new to the platform. This book will get you up to speed quickly with all the information needed to run real-world web applications on Heroku. When using the recipes in this book, it will be helpful to have some prior experience in working with Git and command-line applications.

Sections

In this book, you will find several headings that appear frequently (Getting ready, How to do it, How it works, There's more, and See also). To give clear instructions on how to complete a recipe, we use these sections as follows:

Getting ready

This section tells you what to expect in the recipe, and describes how to set up any software or any preliminary settings required for the recipe.

How to do it...

This section contains the steps required to follow the recipe.

How it works...

This section usually consists of a detailed explanation of what happened in the previous section.

There's more...

This section consists of additional information about the recipe in order to make the reader more knowledgeable about the recipe.

See also

This section provides helpful links to other useful information for the recipe.

Conventions

In this book, you will find a number of styles of text that distinguish between different kinds of information. Here are some examples of these styles and an explanation of their meaning.

Code words in text, database table names, folder names, filenames, file extensions, pathnames, dummy URLs, user input, and Twitter handles are shown as follows: "Make sure the `log-runtime-metrics` plugin is installed and the application was restarted."

A block of code is set as follows:

```
worker_processes Integer(ENV['WEB_CONCURRENCY'] || 2)
timeout Integer(ENV['WEB_TIMEOUT'] || 15)
listen ENV['PORT'], backlog: Integer(ENV['UNICORN_BACKLOG'] || 50)
preload_app true
```

When we wish to draw your attention to a particular part of a code block, the relevant lines or items are set in bold:

```
worker_processes Integer(ENV['WEB_CONCURRENCY'] || 2)
timeout Integer(ENV['WEB_TIMEOUT'] || 15)
listen ENV['PORT'], backlog: Integer(ENV['UNICORN_BACKLOG'] || 50)
preload_app true
```

Any command-line input or output is written as follows:

```
# cp /usr/src/asterisk-addons/configs/cdr_mysql.conf.sample
    /etc/asterisk/cdr_mysql.conf
```

New terms and **important words** are shown in bold. Words that you see on the screen, in menus or dialog boxes for example, appear in the text like this: "We will need to fill in our applications URL and then click on **Load test execution plan**."

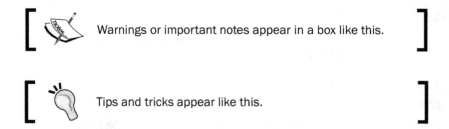

Warnings or important notes appear in a box like this.

Tips and tricks appear like this.

Reader feedback

Feedback from our readers is always welcome. Let us know what you think about this book— what you liked or may have disliked. Reader feedback is important for us to develop titles that you really get the most out of.

To send us general feedback, simply send an e-mail to feedback@packtpub.com, and mention the book title via the subject of your message.

If there is a topic that you have expertise in and you are interested in either writing or contributing to a book, see our author guide on www.packtpub.com/authors.

Customer support

Now that you are the proud owner of a Packt book, we have a number of things to help you to get the most from your purchase.

Downloading the color images of this book

We also provide you a PDF file that has color images of the screenshots/diagrams used in this book. The color images will help you better understand the changes in the output. You can download this file from `http://www.packtpub.com/sites/default/files/downloads/7944OT_ColorImages.pdf`.

Errata

Although we have taken every care to ensure the accuracy of our content, mistakes do happen. If you find a mistake in one of our books—maybe a mistake in the text or the code—we would be grateful if you would report this to us. By doing so, you can save other readers from frustration and help us improve subsequent versions of this book. If you find any errata, please report them by visiting `http://www.packtpub.com/submit-errata`, selecting your book, clicking on the **errata submission form** link, and entering the details of your errata. Once your errata are verified, your submission will be accepted and the errata will be uploaded on our website, or added to any list of existing errata, under the Errata section of that title. Any existing errata can be viewed by selecting your title from `http://www.packtpub.com/support`.

Piracy

Piracy of copyright material on the Internet is an ongoing problem across all media. At Packt, we take the protection of our copyright and licenses very seriously. If you come across any illegal copies of our works, in any form, on the Internet, please provide us with the location address or website name immediately so that we can pursue a remedy.

Please contact us at `copyright@packtpub.com` with a link to the suspected pirated material.

We appreciate your help in protecting our authors, and our ability to bring you valuable content.

Questions

You can contact us at `questions@packtpub.com` if you are having a problem with any aspect of the book, and we will do our best to address it.

1
Getting Started with Heroku

In this chapter, we will cover:

- ▶ Installing the Heroku Toolbelt
- ▶ Introducing version control with Git
- ▶ Deploying a Rails application to Heroku
- ▶ Deploying a Node.js application to Heroku
- ▶ Introducing dynos, workers, and scaling

Introduction

As developers, we work in a world of abstractions. Each piece of technology that we use is built upon layers and layers of other systems. This allows us to build software more efficiently. Why recreate what has already been created? Frameworks such as Ruby on Rails, Django, and Node. js were created to abstract away the painful parts of web development. They set up standards and best practices to build web applications. We have all of these amazing tools to build applications, but for a long time, we still struggled to easily deploy and scale them.

Then came Heroku. Heroku is the Platform as a Service that changed how we deploy web applications. Heroku automates the pain points of deploying code and has established best practices to build applications that need to scale. We no longer need to deal with the pain of setting up load balancers, patching servers, or scrambling to scale up our infrastructure in response to high traffic.

Heroku is easy to get started with and use. For developers who are new to the Heroku way, some of the conventions might go against the ones you use to deploy code. Building scalable and highly performant web applications requires us to think about the design of our applications differently.

In this book, we will learn how to set up our applications for success on Heroku. We'll learn about what is happening behind the scenes and use this knowledge to make our applications fast and reliable from the very beginning.

In this chapter, we will cover the very basics of deploying to Heroku. We will practice deploying three different open source projects, each using a different language and framework. Through this practice, we'll learn the essentials for deploying any application to Heroku and become more confident when it is time for us to deploy our own code.

Installing the Heroku Toolbelt

Heroku applications are created and administered from the command line. To get started with Heroku, we need to install the Heroku Toolbelt. It contains everything we need to create and deploy new applications.

The toolbelt is an installer for three command-line tools:

- **Heroku Command Line Interface (CLI)**: This is an interface to the Heroku Platform API
- **Git**: This is used for version control and to deploy our applications
- **Foreman**: This is a tool to run Procfile-based applications

In this recipe, we will install the Heroku Toolbelt, making sure our machine is set up to use the Heroku CLI. We'll also be briefly introduced to the Heroku CLI. We'll learn about Git and Foreman later in the chapter.

 If you already have the Heroku Toolbelt, it might be beneficial to go through the following steps again to ensure that the latest version is installed.

Getting ready

First, we need to create a Heroku account with the following steps:

1. Let's go to www.heroku.com and create an account if we do not already have one.

Remember to use a strong and unique password for Heroku. This account will be able to access our source code and data, so treat it like any other sensitive set of credentials.

2. Next, let's install the Heroku Toolbelt. Specific download and installation instructions are available at `https://toolbelt.heroku.com/` for Mac, Windows, and Linux.

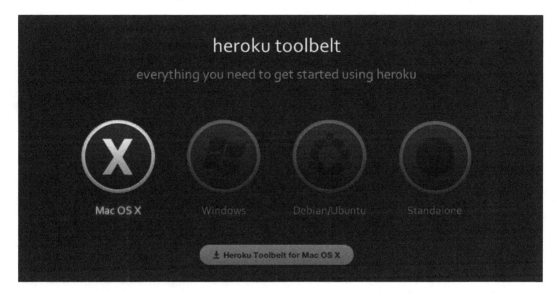

 Throughout this book, we will be using a $ sign to indicate that a command should be run in a terminal. The $ sign is not part of the command.

3. Once the Heroku Toolbelt is installed, we can verify that everything is working by opening up a terminal and running the following command:

```
$ heroku --version
heroku-toolbelt/3.11.1 (x86_64-darwin10.8.0) ruby/1.9.3
```

We should see the version of the Heroku Toolbelt we are using printed to the console.

How to do it...

Now that we have the Heroku Toolbelt installed, let's log in to our account via the CLI and authorize our computer by uploading our public key using the following steps:

1. Let's log in by opening up a terminal and running the following command:

   ```
   $ heroku login
   Username: youremail@example.com
   Password (typing will be hidden):
   Could not find an existing public key.
   Would you like to generate one? [Yn]
   Generating new SSH public key.
   Uploading ssh public key /Users/mc/.ssh/id_rsa.pub
   ```

   If we do not have an existing public key, the Heroku CLI will provide us with instructions on how to create one here. This key will be uploaded to Heroku's servers and used for authentication whenever we push new code to our applications.

    We'll need to repeat this step for any other computers we use Heroku from.

2. We can ensure that we are authenticated with the `auth:whoami` command. If logged in successfully, it will print our e-mail address:

   ```
   $ heroku auth:whoami
   ```
   ```
   youremail@example.com
   ```

3. Finally, we should go to the Heroku dashboard and verify our account by adding a credit card. Having a verified account will allow us to scale our applications and install add-ons (`https://dashboard.heroku.com/account`).

How it works...

The Heroku Toolbelt installs all the necessary tools to create and administer our Heroku applications. It's essential for us to become comfortable with Heroku's command-line tools. Even though many tasks can be completed on Heroku's website, not everything is available through the dashboard. For full control over our applications, we have to use the CLI.

Authentication

Ever wondered how Heroku keeps us logged in to the CLI? During the login process, Heroku stores an API key for our account in our `.netrc` file. The `.netrc` file is a dotfile that lives in our home directory. It's a common file that applications use to store credentials to log in to remote hosts. The API key stored in this file is used for subsequent logins and keeps us logged in to our Heroku account. If we open our `.netrc` file, we'll see an entry for `api.heroku.com`. If we ever run the `auth:logout` command, it deletes the entry from our `.netrc` file, thus logging us out.

 We do not need to worry about updating Heroku Toolbelt; it will automatically check for updates for us.

See also

▶ Interested in seeing the source code for the Heroku CLI? It's open source; take a look at `https://github.com/heroku/heroku`.

Introducing version control with Git

Git is one of the most popular version-control systems used in software development. It allows teams of developers to work on the same code base without overwriting each other's changes. Git is a core piece of the Heroku platform, and having a basic understanding of how it works is a prerequisite to deploy code to Heroku.

In this recipe, we'll learn enough about Git to deploy code to Heroku.

 Unfamiliar with the command line? There is a great resource to quickly get up to speed on the basics at `http://cli.learncodethehardway.org/book/`.

How to do it...

Git allows us to track every change to our source code. This makes it simple to go back in time and revert changes as well as view the history of our code. Let's open up a terminal to get started by performing the following steps:

1. If we've never used Git before, we'll want to tell it our name and e-mail. These will be used to identify us as the author in all our commits:

```
$ git config --global user.name 'First and Last name here'
$ git config --global user.email 'yourname@example.com'
```

2. Now, let's create a new directory to practice with:

```
$ mkdir LearningGit
$ cd LearningGit
```

3. In our new directory, we'll need to initialize a new Git repository:

```
$ git init
Initialized empty Git repository in /home/mc/LearningGit/.git/
```

4. Now, let's create a new file in our project using `touch`:

```
$ touch new_file.txt
```

5. We can use the `status` command to check whether this file is currently untracked by Git:

```
$ git status
On branch master

Initial commit

Untracked files:
    (use "git add <file>..." to include in what will be committed)

        new_file.txt

nothing added to commit but untracked files present (use "git add"
to track)
```

 The default output of the Git status can be a little verbose. Use `git status -sb` for a more concise output.

6. We need to explicitly tell Git to track the file using the `add` command:

```
$ git add new_file.txt
```

 Try to run `git status` again. See the difference?

7. Our file is now created and being tracked by Git, but it is not yet committed to our repository's history. Let's commit it now:

```
$ git commit -m "Adding new_file to Git"
[master (root-commit) b79ca0b] Adding new_file to Git
1 file changed, 0 insertions(+), 0 deletions(-)
create mode 100644 LearningGit/new_file.txt
```

 To save time, we can combine `git add` and `git commit` in a single command. The `git commit -am` command will stage any currently tracked files and commit them.

8. To view the history of our Git repository, we can use the `log` command. Use the *q* key to escape from viewing logs. Use the arrow keys to scroll:

```
$ git log
commit b79ca0b7c7671789cc8359fe43e1144af835c2d1
Author: Mike Coutermarsh <coutermarsh.mike@gmail.com>
Date:   Mon Mar 3 20:31:47 2014 -0500

    Adding new_file to Git
```

We now know the essential commands to use Git from the command line. We're able to create a new repository, add and track the files, as well as view our repositories' status and history. These are just a limited set of Git's commands, but they are enough for us to get started with Heroku. We'll be using Git throughout this book to track and push our code. We'll build on the skills we learned here in the later recipes.

How it works...

An easy way to understand Git commits is to think of each commit as a photograph of our project files. Each time we make a commit, Git takes a photo of our files. We are then able to view each commit to see exactly what changed in our project. If we need to go back in time, we can just revert to the state our code was in before the commit was made.

Git is a distributed version-control system. This means that there is no need for us to be online or connected to a server to use it. In Git, there is the concept of **remotes**. These are other instances of the Git repository on other servers or machines. If we have a Git repository on GitHub, then this is known as a remote. Having remotes is useful because they act as a central place where all the members of a team can push their changes and retrieve the changes made by others. Having the full Git repository on multiple machines and servers also makes it much more fault tolerant. If anything were to happen to our remote repository, each team member would still have a local copy that can be used to create a new remote elsewhere.

Remotes are an important concept for us to understand because they are the basis to deploy to Heroku. Each Heroku deploy is simply the push of a local Git repository to a remote provided by Heroku. It's amazingly simple; we'll learn about it in detail later in this chapter.

There's more...

Using and learning about Git from the command line can be challenging. Luckily, there are a few easy-to-use desktop apps that make using Git really simple:

- ▶ GitHub for Mac available at `http://mac.github.com/`
- ▶ GitHub for Windows available at `http://windows.github.com/`
- ▶ SourceTree (Mac or Windows) available at `http://www.sourcetreeapp.com/`
- ▶ Tower (Mac) available at `http://www.git-tower.com/`
- ▶ SmartGit (Linux) available at `http://www.syntevo.com/smartgithg/`

See also

- ▶ Grab the Git cheatsheet at `http://cheat.errtheblog.com/s/git`
- ▶ For an interactive tutorial on using Git, check out TryGit at `https://try.github.io`
- ▶ Packt has a great beginner's guide to using Git, *Git: Version Control for Everyone*, *Ravishankar Somasundaram*

Deploying a Rails application to Heroku

It's time for us to deploy our first application to Heroku. If you've deployed applications to Heroku before, this will be a good review. If this is your first time, you'll be learning the common steps taken to deploy any application to Heroku.

The creators of Heroku have experience in deploying and scaling countless web applications. They've seen it all. From their experiences, they have created a methodology known as the Twelve-Factor app. The Twelve-Factor app is a set of 12 rules that will guide us to build an application that is easy to deploy, easy to maintain, and, most importantly, easy to scale on a cloud platform. No matter what language or framework we are using to build our application, these twelve rules will apply.

 Visit `http://12factor.net/` to learn more about the Twelve-Factor app.

Ruby on Rails follows most of the twelve rules out of the box. This makes it a good place to start when learning how to deploy to Heroku, because it requires minor configuration changes. In this recipe, we will be deploying Refinery, a popular open source Ruby on Rails **Content Management System** (**CMS**).

Getting ready

To run this application locally, we need to have Ruby Version 2.1.3 installed by performing the following steps:

1. One of the easiest ways to install Ruby is to use **Ruby Version Manager** (**RVM**). We can find the latest installation instructions for RVM at http://rvm.io/rvm/install.

2. Once RVM is installed, we can run the following command in a terminal to install Ruby 2.1.3:

   ```
   $ rvm install 2.1.3
   ```

3. We'll use **Bundler** to manage and install our applications' dependencies. Let's make sure we have the latest version installed by running the following command:

   ```
   $ gem install bundler
   ```

4. This application also uses a Postgres database. We'll be using Postgres frequently throughout the book; if we do not have it installed on our machine, now is a good time to get it set up:
   - For OS X, the easiest way to install Postgres is via the Postgres app available at http://postgresapp.com/
   - For Windows and Linux, see the Postgres download page at http://www.postgresql.org/download/

How to do it...

We'll set up and deploy our application from the command line. Let's open a terminal to get started using the following steps:

1. First, we need to download the source code for our sample app from GitHub. We can do this using git clone:

   ```
   $ git clone https://github.com/mscoutermarsh/refinery_heroku.git
   ```

2. Now, let's navigate to our new directory and create a new Heroku app. Creating a new app will also add a new heroku remote to our Git repository. This remote is where we will be soon pushing our code for deployment:

   ```
   $ cd refinery_heroku
   $ heroku apps:create
   ```

```
Creating cryptic-chamber-6830... done, stack is cedar
http://cryptic-chamber-6830.herokuapp.com/ | git@heroku.
com:cryptic-chamber-6830.git
Git remote heroku added
```

 Heroku automatically generates an app name for us. If we want to specify our app name, we can add our app name to the end of the command (`$ heroku apps:create my_app_name`).

3. We will tell Heroku how to run our app with a Procfile. In the root directory of our new app, we'll create a new Procfile to tell Heroku how to start up our web service. Let's create the file using the `touch` command:

   `$ touch Procfile`

4. Now, let's open our new Procfile and add the following line. This will tell Heroku how to start our web server process:

   ```
   web: bundle exec unicorn -p $PORT -c ./config/unicorn.rb
   ```

    `$PORT` in this command is an environment variable that Heroku will manage for us. It determines the port that our web server will run on.

5. We can now commit these changes to Git:

   `$ git add Procfile`

   `$ git commit -m 'Adding Procfile for Heroku'`

    For an example of what the Procfile should look like, one has already been added to this example application. Take a look at `Procfile.example` in the root directory of the project.

6. Next, let's add the Twelve-Factor app gem to our application. It will automatically configure our application's logging and assets to work correctly with Heroku. Let's open our application's Gemfile and add the following line:

   `gem 'rails_12factor', group: :production`

7. As we've added a new gem, we'll want to run `bundle install` to update our application's dependencies:

   `$ bundle install`

To learn more about Bundler, take a look at `http://bundler.io/`.

8. We'll need to make another commit with our latest changes:

```
$ git commit -am 'Adding 12 factor gem'
```

 We are able to use the -am flag here because Git is already tracking the files we are committing.

9. This application uses a Postgres database. We'll need to add Postgres to our Heroku application. Let's do this now:

```
$ heroku addons:add heroku-postgresql:dev

----> Adding heroku-postgresql:dev to cryptic-chamber-6830...
done, v3 (free)
        Attached as HEROKU_POSTGRESQL_GOLD_URL
        Database has been created and is available
        ! This database is empty. If upgrading, you can transfer
        ! data from another database with pgbackups:restore.
```

 The Heroku CLI knows which application to add the database to, because our current Git repository has a `heroku` remote that points to this Heroku application. If we wanted to run the command for a different application, we could append `--app application_name` to the end of the command. This will be very useful once we have multiple applications deployed to Heroku.

10. Ruby on Rails uses an environment variable to connect to the database. We can set this now using the `promote` command. This will assign our new database's credentials to the `DATABASE_URL` environment variable.

    We'll use the database name given to us in the previous command as the argument in this command:

```
$ heroku pg:promote HEROKU_POSTGRESQL_GOLD

-----> Promoting HEROKU_POSTGRESQL_GOLD to DATABASE_URL... done
```

 It's good practice to keep all the credentials in environment variables. This is part of the Twelve-Factor app.

11. We're now ready to push our code to Heroku. We'll do this using Git's `push` command. We'll need to specify the `heroku` remote and our master Git branch:

```
$ git push heroku master
Initializing repository, done.
Counting objects: 92, done.
Delta compression using up to 4 threads.
Compressing objects: 100% (79/79), done.
Writing objects: 100% (92/92), 35.83 KiB | 0 bytes/s, done.
Total 92 (delta 11), reused 0 (delta 0)


...


-----> Discovering process types
       Procfile declares types -> web
       Default types for Ruby  -> console, rake, worker

-----> Compressing... done, 37.1MB
-----> Launching... done, v9
       http://cryptic-chamber-6830.herokuapp.com/ deployed to
Heroku

To git@heroku.com:cryptic-chamber-6830.git
   46345bc..583680c  master -> master
```

> We can always see a list of our available Git remotes by running `$ git remote -v`.
>
> During the deploy process, our app will compile all of our application's style sheets and JavaScript. This might take a few minutes; Refinery has a lot of assets.

12. Now that our application's code is on Heroku, we need to completely set up our database by running migrations and seeding it with some data:

```
$ heroku run rake db:migrate
$ heroku run rake db:seed
```

The `heroku run` command is equivalent to SSHing into a server and running a command.

13. Our app is now ready to use! We can quickly launch a browser and view it with the `open` command:

    ```
    $ heroku open
    ```

 By default, all Heroku applications have an `application-name.herokuapp.com` domain name. This domain directs requests to the web server we defined in our Procfile.

14. Once our application is open, let's go to Refinery in the browser to register a user and start using the Refinery CMS.

How it works...

In deploying this Rails application, we were introduced to a couple of Heroku concepts that we will be using when deploying any application to Heroku. Let's dig into them a little deeper now.

The Procfile

Each Heroku application should have a special file in its root directory that defines each of the processes required to run the application. This file is known as a Procfile. If we forget to include a Procfile, Heroku will try to guess what process we want to run. It's better for us if we're explicit about exactly what Heroku should do.

In this recipe, we created a Procfile that told Heroku what command to run to start our web server. The Procfile can be used for more than just web processes. In applications that also have processes running in the background, the Procfile is where we'd define how to start them. On Heroku, we can only have one web process. This is the only process that Heroku will direct web traffic to. Other processes will not be able to receive web traffic. If we find a use case where we need more than one type of web process running, this is a good indicator that we should have multiple Heroku applications.

Environment variables

When we ran the `db:promote` command, we added an environment variable to our application to store our database's credentials. This is good practice and follows the conventions of the Twelve-Factor app. We should never store credentials for any service in our Git repository. It makes our credentials less secure, because they are then accessible to anyone who works on our code. It also makes them more difficult to change, because any change will require another deploy. Credentials tend to be very environment specific; having them as part of a Heroku application rather than our code base makes our application more portable. With all this being said, the key is to remember that when building any application for deployment on Heroku, we should build the ability to load credentials from an environment variable into our code.

The build process

When we pushed our Git repository to Heroku, the slug compilation process began. Heroku takes our Git repository, detects the language and the framework used, and begins to build a slug in our application. A Heroku slug is a copy of our application that is ready to be deployed on Heroku's servers at a moment's notice. For a Rails application, this means that all of the application's Gems have been installed, and its assets have been compiled. Heroku also removes any unnecessary files from our Git repository to make the slug as lightweight as possible. We can think of it as a snapshot of our production-ready application. Heroku hangs on to each slug it creates, making it easy for us to roll back to a previous slug if needed.

See also

- Find out more about the Refinery CMS at `http://refinerycms.com/`
- Find out more about Foreman and the Procfile at `http://ddollar.github.io/foreman/`
- To learn more about deploying Ruby applications on Heroku, take a look at *Chapter 7, Optimizing Ruby Server Performance on Heroku*

Deploying a Node.js application to Heroku

Heroku is a polyglot platform that can host applications built in many different languages and frameworks. In this recipe, we will learn how to deploy Ghost, a popular open source blogging platform built on Node.js.

We'll build on what we learned in the previous recipe, *Deploying a Rails application to Heroku*. Here, we'll see that there are a lot of similarities between deploying the two different applications. The process to deploy any application to Heroku is very similar to the previous recipe, irrespective of the language or framework in which it is written.

How to do it...

We'll be setting up and deploying Ghost from the command line. Let's open up a terminal to begin with by performing the following steps:

1. First, we'll need to download the Ghost source code from GitHub. We'll clone an existing Ghost Git repository that's been set up to run on Heroku:

    ```
    $ git clone https://github.com/mscoutermarsh/ghost_heroku.git
    Cloning into 'ghost_heroku'...
    remote: Counting objects: 16411, done.
    remote: Compressing objects: 100% (7480/7480), done.
    remote: Total 16411 (delta 8481), reused 16381 (delta 8455)
    Receiving objects: 100% (16411/16411), 8.55 MiB | 1.75 MiB/s,
    done.
    Resolving deltas: 100% (8481/8481), done.
    Checking connectivity... done
    ```

     This specific Ghost repository was set up to be easy to deploy to Heroku. The difference between this repository and the core Ghost source code is that it has a Procfile added and the configuration has been set up to use a Postgres connection defined by an environment variable.

2. Let's navigate to the new `ghost_heroku` directory and create a new Heroku application:

    ```
    $ cd ghost_heroku
    $ heroku apps:create
    Creating fast-coast-3773... done, region is us
    http://fast-coast-3773.herokuapp.com/ |
    ```

```
git@heroku.com:fast-coast-3773.git
Git remote heroku added
```

3. The configuration for our application is in the `config.js` file. Let's open the file now and update the default production URL to reflect our new Heroku application's URL (given to us from Heroku in the previous step):

```
production: {
  url: 'http://my-ghost-blog.com',
  mail: {},
```

4. Commit the changes to Git:

```
$ git commit -am 'Updating production URL config'
[master cd0ec0e] Updating production URL config
 1 file changed, 1 insertion(+), 1 deletion(-)
```

5. We'll use Postgres as our database for Ghost. We can create a new Postgres database now:

```
$ heroku addons:add heroku-postgresql:dev
 Adding heroku-postgresql:dev on fast-coast-3773... done, v3
(free)
 Attached as HEROKU_POSTGRESQL_SILVER_URL
 Database has been created and is available
  ! This database is empty. If upgrading, you can transfer
  ! data from another database with pgbackups:restore.
 Use `heroku addons:docs heroku-postgresql:dev` to view
documentation.
```

6. We'll need to set up our new database as the primary one for our application by promoting it. In the previous command, Heroku gave us a unique database name. It follows the format of HEROKU_POSTGRESQL_COLOR_URL. We'll use that name as the argument for the next command:

```
$ heroku pg:promote HEROKU_POSTGRESQL_SILVER_URL
 Promoting HEROKU_POSTGRESQL_SILVER_URL to DATABASE_URL... done
```

 Our Ghost installation is set up to parse Heroku's DATABASE_URL to connect to the database. To see how this works, look at the production database section of `config.js`.

7. Next, we'll need to set a configuration variable to let Node know which environment it's running on. Let's set it to `production`:

```
$ heroku config:set NODE_ENV=production
```

 The terms *environment variable* and *configuration variable* are interchangeable.

8. Our application now has everything it needs to be deployed. Let's push our repository to Heroku to deploy our code:

```
$ git push heroku master
```

 Heroku only deploys code in the master branch of our Git repository. If we want to deploy a code from a different branch, we can use the `$ git push heroku other_branch_name:master` command.

9. Once the build process is complete, our blog will be up and running. We can now launch a browser from the command line to see the following screen:

```
$ heroku open
```

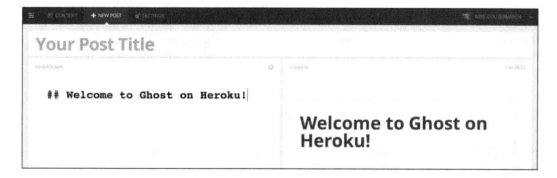

10. To access Ghost's admin panel, add `/ghost` at the end of the URL. We can then create an account and start playing with our new blog.

How it works...

Heroku uses a unique term for its web servers; it calls them **dynos**. A dyno starts out as a plain Ubuntu Linux web server. It's during the initial push and slug-compilation process that Heroku auto detects the type of application we are trying to deploy and installs the software necessary for it to run.

The ephemeral filesystem

Heroku uses an ephemeral filesystem. This means that any files written to disk after the creation of the slug will not be persisted beyond the life of the dyno. All Heroku dynos are cycled every 24 hours. There is a good reason for this restriction: it allows our application to scale. If we were to allow file storage on Heroku dynos, we'd have to replicate the file across every dyno.

When writing blog posts with Ghost, we'll see that we are able to upload images. The problem with this feature is that Ghost currently stores these images on the web server. This won't work for us on Heroku; we'll have to use a file store outside Heroku, such as Amazon S3 or Dropbox.

See also

- ▶ See `ghost.org` to learn more about Ghost
- ▶ Check out the Ghost project on GitHub at `https://github.com/tryghost/Ghost`

Introducing dynos, workers, and scaling

Heroku's killer feature has always been its ability to easily scale up and scale out our applications as our user base grows. This frees us from the pains of setting up and managing load balancers and additional servers on our own. In this recipe, we will be introduced to Heroku's dynos and workers as well as learn how to scale them both up and out as our applications grow.

> **Scaling up** and **scaling out** are two common terms used when growing web applications:
>
> - ▶ **Scaling up** (vertical scaling) means that we are making our servers more powerful by adding more CPU/RAM
> - ▶ **Scaling out** (horizontal scaling) means that we are adding more servers to our application

What's a dyno?

Dyno is the term Heroku uses for its web servers. A dyno is simply a virtual private server that runs our application and responds to web requests.

> Heroku provides us with one free 1X dyno per month. This is useful for testing and development.

What's a worker?

Heroku has an additional class of servers known as **workers**. These are identical to dynos, with the exception that they do not serve web requests.

Process sizes

Both dynos and workers are available in three different sizes: 1X, 2X, and PX. The default size is 1X; this is a small virtual server with 512 MB of RAM. These are large enough to run most web applications. However, if we find that our application is constrained by the limited memory or CPU size, we can scale up our dynos up to 2X, which provides 1024 MB of RAM and twice as much computing power.

 If our application has only a single 1X dyno running, it will shut down after an hour of inactivity. To avoid this, we need to have at least two dynos running or use a single 2X dyno.

The largest process size is the PX or performance dyno. These are dedicated virtual servers that do not share resources with any other Heroku customers. They have 6 GB of RAM and 40 times the compute resources of the standard 1X-sized dyno. Performance dynos should only be considered for applications that have high memory and CPU requirements.

 Heads up! Performance dynos are expensive, so don't accidently leave one running.

How to do it...

We'll use the Heroku CLI for this recipe. Let's open up a terminal and navigate to a directory with one of our existing Heroku applications and perform the following steps:

1. To view our currently running processes, we can use the `ps` command. It will show the type, the size, and exactly what's running:

    ```
    $ heroku ps
    === web (1X): `bundle exec unicorn -p $PORT -c ./config/unicorn.
    rb`
    web.1: up 2014/03/15 19:41:27 (~ 8s ago)
    ```

2. We currently have only one dyno running for this application. Let's scale it up to two; this will effectively double our application's capacity. Scaling processes are done with the `ps:scale` command:

    ```
    $ heroku ps:scale web=2
    Scaling dynos... done, now running web at 2:1X.
    ```

3. The `scale` command is very flexible. If we want, we can scale both dynos and workers at the same time:

```
$ heroku ps:scale web=2 worker=1

Scaling dynos... done, now running worker at 1:1X, web at 2:1X.
```

 We can run these commands on any of our applications by including `--app app_name` at the end of the command.

4. We can change the size of our dynos using `ps:resize`. Let's scale up our web dynos to 2X:

```
$ heroku ps:resize web=2x

Resizing and restarting the specified dynos... done

web dynos now 2X ($0.10/dyno-hour)
```

5. We can also scale and change the size in the same command. Let's dial our dynos back down to one and adjust the size to 1X:

```
$ heroku ps:scale web=1:1x

Scaling dynos... done, now running web at 1:1X.
```

 The name of the process we are scaling depends on what is in our application's Procfile. In these examples, our processes are named `web` and `worker`. Web processes are the only ones that Heroku will send web traffic to. We can name our other processes anything we like.

6. To finish up, we can scale our workers back down to zero:

```
$ heroku ps:scale worker=0

Scaling dynos... done, now running worker at 0:1X.
```

How it works...

Now that we have learned how to scale our applications, let's go a little more in depth to learn about the different types of Heroku dynos.

Dynos

A dyno is simply a web server. When we create our application's Procfile, the web process that we define is what runs on our dynos. When a user visits our web application, their requests get sent to our dynos via Heroku's routing layer. The routing layer acts like a load balancer. It distributes our users' requests and monitors the health of our dynos. To handle more users, we can scale out our application by increasing the number of running dynos. This allows us to serve requests from more concurrent users. If we are currently running one dyno and adding another, we have theoretically doubled the amount of web requests that our application can respond do.

Workers

In our Procfile, any process other than `web` will run on a worker. Workers are used to process background tasks such as sending out e-mails or generating PDFs. Any task that a user should not have to wait for is a good candidate that will run on a worker. For a Rails application, any background job (such as Resque or Sidekiq) will need to be run on a worker dyno. Workers can be scaled in exactly the same way as dynos. If our application has a large backlog of tasks that need to be completed, we can add additional workers to increase the number of tasks we can complete simultaneously.

One-time dynos

When we use `heroku run` to execute a command on our application, Heroku spins up a new dyno specifically to run the command. It's called a one-time dyno. Once the command is complete, it will shut itself down.

See also

▸ To learn more about scaling, take a look at *Chapter 6, Load Testing a Heroku Application*

2
Managing Heroku from the Command Line

In this chapter, we will cover:

- ▶ Viewing application logs
- ▶ Searching logs
- ▶ Installing add-ons
- ▶ Managing environment variables
- ▶ Enabling the maintenance page
- ▶ Managing releases and rolling back
- ▶ Running one-off tasks and dynos
- ▶ Managing SSH keys
- ▶ Sharing and collaboration
- ▶ Monitoring load average and memory usage

Introduction

Heroku was built to be managed from its command-line interface. The better we learn it, the faster and more effective we will be in administering our application. The goal of this chapter is to get comfortable with using the CLI. We'll see that each Heroku command follows a common pattern. Once we learn a few of these commands, the rest will be relatively simple to master.

In this chapter, we won't cover every command available in the CLI, but we will focus on the ones that we'll be using the most. As we learn each command, we will also learn a little more about what is happening behind the scenes so that we get a better understanding of how Heroku works. The more we understand, the more we'll be able to take advantage of the platform.

Before we start, let's note that if we ever need to get a list of the available commands, we can run the following command:

```
$ heroku help
```

We can also quickly display the documentation for a single command:

```
$ heroku help command_name
```

Viewing application logs

Logging gets a little more complex for any application that is running multiple servers and several different types of processes. Having visibility into everything that is happening within our application is critical to maintaining it. Heroku handles this by combining and sending all of our logs to one place, the **Logplex**.

The Logplex provides us with a single location to view a stream of our logs across our entire application. In this recipe, we'll learn how to view logs via the CLI. We'll learn how to quickly get visibility into what's happening within our application.

 We'll learn more about the Logplex and how to set up log storage in *Chapter 5, Error Monitoring and Logging Tools*.

How to do it...

To start, let's open up a terminal, navigate to an existing Heroku application, and perform the following steps:

1. First, to view our applications logs, we can use the `logs` command:

   ```
   $ heroku logs
   2014-03-31T23:35:51.195150+00:00 app[web.1]:    Rendered pages/
   about.html.slim within layouts/application (25.0ms)

   2014-03-31T23:35:51.215591+00:00 app[web.1]:    Rendered layouts/_
   navigation_links.html.erb (2.6ms)

   2014-03-31T23:35:51.230010+00:00 app[web.1]:    Rendered layouts/_
   messages.html.slim (13.0ms)
   ```

```
2014-03-31T23:35:51.215967+00:00 app[web.1]:    Rendered layouts/_
navigation.html.slim (10.3ms)

2014-03-31T23:35:51.231104+00:00 app[web.1]: Completed 200 OK in
109ms (Views: 65.4ms | ActiveRecord: 0.0ms)

2014-03-31T23:35:51.242960+00:00 heroku[router]: at=info
method=GET path=
```

 Heroku logs anything that our application sends to STDOUT or STDERR. If we're not seeing logs, it's very likely our application is not configured correctly.

2. We can also watch our logs in real time. This is known as tailing:

```
$ heroku logs --tail
```

 Instead of --tail, we can also use -t.

We'll need to press *Ctrl + C* to end the command and stop tailing the logs.

3. If we want to see the 100 most recent lines, we can use -n:

```
$ heroku logs -n 100
```

 The Logplex stores a maximum of 1500 lines. To view more lines, we'll have to set up a log storage. We'll learn how to do this in *Chapter 5, Error Monitoring and Logging Tools*.

4. We can filter the logs to only show a specific process type. Here, we will only see logs from our web dynos:

```
$ heroku logs -p web
```

5. If we want, we can be as granular as showing the logs from an individual dyno. This will show only the logs from the second web dyno:

```
$ heroku logs -p web.2
```

6. We can use this for any process type; we can try it for our workers if we'd like:

```
$ heroku logs -p worker
```

7. The Logplex contains more than just logs from our application. We can also view logs generated by Heroku or the API. Let's try changing the source to Heroku to only see the logs generated by Heroku. This will only show us logs related to the router and resource usage:

```
$ heroku logs --source heroku
```

8. To view logs for only our application, we can set the source to `app`:

```
$ heroku logs --source app
```

9. We can also view logs from the API. These logs will show any administrative actions we've taken, such as scaling dynos or changing configuration variables. This can be useful when multiple developers are working on an application:

```
$ heroku logs --source api
```

10. We can even combine the different flags. Let's try tailing the logs for only our web dynos:

```
$ heroku logs -p web --tail
```

11. That's it! Remember that if we ever need more information on how to view logs via the CLI, we can always use the `help` command:

```
$ heroku help logs
```

How it works

Under the covers, the Heroku CLI simply passes our request to Heroku's API and then uses Ruby to parse and display our logs. If you're interested in exactly how it works, the code is open source on GitHub at `https://github.com/heroku/heroku/blob/master/lib/heroku/command/logs.rb`.

Viewing logs via the CLI is most useful in situations where we need to see exactly what our application is doing right now. We'll find that we use it a lot around deploys and when debugging issues. Since the Logplex has a limit of 1500 lines, it's not meant to view any historical data. For this, we'll need to set up log drains and enable a logging add-on. We'll be learning how to do this in *Chapter 5, Error Monitoring and Logging Tools*.

See also

▶ To learn how to keep and search historical logs, take a look at *Chapter 5, Error Monitoring and Logging Tools*

Searching logs

Heroku does not have the built-in capability to search our logs from the command line. We can get around this limitation easily by making use of some other command-line tools.

In this recipe, we will learn how to combine Heroku's logs with Grep, a command-line tool to search text. This will allow us to search our recent logs for keywords, helping us track down errors more quickly.

Getting ready

For this recipe, we'll need to have Grep installed. For OS X and Linux machines, it should already be installed. We can install Grep using the following steps:

1. To check if we have Grep installed, let's open up a terminal and type the following:

```
$ grep
usage: grep [-abcDEFGHhIiJLlmnOoPqRSsUVvwxZ] [-A num] [-B num]
[-C[num]]
        [-e pattern] [-f file] [--binary-files=value]
[--color=when]
        [--context[=num]] [--directories=action] [--label]
[--line-buffered]
        [--null] [pattern] [file ...]
```

2. If we do not see usage instructions, we can visit http://www.gnu.org/software/grep/ for the download and installation instructions.

How to do it...

Let's start searching our logs by opening a terminal and navigating to one of our Heroku applications using the following steps:

1. To search for a keyword in our logs, we need to pipe our logs into Grep. This simply means that we will be passing our logs into Grep and having Grep search them for us. Let's try this now. The following command will search the output of heroku logs for the word error:

```
$ heroku logs | grep error
```

2. Sometimes, we might want to search for a longer string that includes special characters. We can do this by surrounding it with quotes:

```
$ heroku logs | grep "path=/pages/about host"
```

3. It can be useful to also see the lines surrounding the line that matched our search. We can do this as well. The next command will show us the line that contains an error as well as the three lines above and below it:

```
$ heroku logs | grep error -C 3
```

4. We can even search with regular expressions. The next command will show us every line that matches a number that ends with MB. So, for example, lines with 100 MB, 25 MB, or 3 MB will all appear:

```
$ heroku logs | grep '\d*MB'
```

To learn more about regular expressions, visit `http://regex.learncodethehardway.org/`.

How it works...

Like most Unix-based tools, Grep was built to accomplish a single task and to do it well. **Global regular expression print (Grep)** is built to search a set of files for a pattern and then print all of the matches.

Grep can also search anything it receives through standard input; this is exactly how we used it in this recipe. By piping the output of our Heroku logs into Grep, we are passing our logs to Grep as standard input.

See also

▶   To learn more about Grep, visit `http://www.tutorialspoint.com/unix_commands/grep.htm`

Installing add-ons

Our application needs some additional functionality provided by an outside service. What should we do? In the past, this would have involved creating accounts, managing credentials, and maybe even bringing up servers and installing software. This whole process has been simplified by the Heroku add-on marketplace.

For any additional functionality that our application needs, our first stop should always be Heroku add-ons. Heroku has made attaching additional resources to our application a plug-and-play process. If we need an additional database, caching, or error logging, they can be set up with a single command.

In this recipe, we will learn the ins and outs of using the Heroku CLI to install and manage our application's add-ons.

How to do it...

To begin, let's open a terminal and navigate to one of our Heroku applications using the following steps:

1.   Let's start by taking a look at all of the available Heroku add-ons. We can do this with the `addons:list` command:

```
$ heroku addons:list
```

There are so many add-ons that viewing them through the CLI is pretty difficult. For easier navigation and search, we should take a look at `https://addons.heroku.com/`.

2. If we want to see the currently installed add-ons for our application, we can simply type the following:

```
$ heroku addons
=== load-tester-rails Configured Add-ons
heroku-postgresql:dev          HEROKU_POSTGRESQL_MAROON
heroku-postgresql:hobby-dev    HEROKU_POSTGRESQL_ONYX
librato:development
newrelic:stark
```

 Remember that for any command, we can always add `--app app_name` to specify the application.

3. Alternatively, our application's add-ons are also listed through the Heroku Dashboard available at `https://dashboard.heroku.com`.

Add-ons

Deploy Hooks	HipChat Hook
MemCachier	Developer
New Relic	Stark
PG Backups	Plus
Redis To Go	Nano
+ Get more addons...	

4. The installation of a new add-on is done with `addons:add`. Here, we are going to install the error logging service, Rollbar:

```
$ heroku addons:add rollbar
heroku addons:add rollbar
Adding rollbar on load-tester-rails... done, v22 (free)
Use `heroku addons:docs rollbar` to view documentation.
```

5. We can quickly open up the documentation for an add-on with `addons:docs`:

```
$ heroku addons:docs rollbar
```

6. Removing an add-on is just as simple. We'll need to type our application name to confirm. For this example, our application is called `load-tester-rails`:

```
$ heroku addons:remove rollbar


 !      WARNING: Destructive Action
 !      This command will affect the app: load-tester-rails
 !      To proceed, type "load-tester-rails" or re-run this command
with --confirm load-tester-rails


> load-tester-rails
Removing rollbar on load-tester-rails... done, v23 (free)
```

7. Each add-on comes with different tiers of service. Let's try upgrading our `rollbar` add-on to the starter tier:

```
$ heroku addons:upgrade rollbar:starter
Upgrading to rollbar:starter on load-tester-rails... done, v26
($12/mo)
Plan changed to starter
Use `heroku addons:docs rollbar` to view documentation.
```

8. Now, if we want, we can downgrade back to its original level with `addons:downgrade`:

```
$ heroku addons:downgrade rollbar
Downgrading to rollbar on load-tester-rails... done, v27 (free)
Plan changed to free
Use `heroku addons:docs rollbar` to view documentation.
```

9. If we ever forget any of the commands, we can always use `help` to quickly see the documentation:

```
$ heroku help addons
```

 Some add-ons might charge you money. Before continuing, let's double check that we only have the correct ones enabled, using the $ `heroku addons` command.

How it works...

Heroku has created a standardized process for all add-on providers to follow. This ensures a consistent experience when provisioning any add-ons for our application.

It starts when we request the creation of an add-on. Heroku sends an HTTP request to the provider, asking them to provision an instance of their service. The provider must then respond to Heroku with the connection details for their service in the form of environment variables. For example, if we were to provision Redis To Go, we will get back our connection details in a `REDISTOGO_URL` variable:

```
REDISTOGO_URL: redis://user:pass@server.redistogo.com:9652
```

Heroku adds these variables to our application and restarts it. On restart, the variables are available for our application, and we can connect to the service using them. The specifics on how to connect using the variables will be in the add-ons documentation. Installation will depend on the specific language or framework we're using.

See also

- ▶ For details on creating our own add-ons, the process is well documented on Heroku's website at `https://addons.heroku.com/provider`
- ▶ Check out Kensa, the CLI to create Heroku add-ons, at `https://github.com/heroku/kensa`

Managing environment variables

Our applications will often need access to various credentials in the form of API tokens, usernames, and passwords for integrations with third-party services. We can store this information in our Git repository, but then, anyone with access to our code will also have a copy of our production credentials. We should instead use environment variables to store any configuration information for our application. Configuration information should be separate from our application's code and instead be tied to the specific deployment of the application.

Changing our application to use environment variables is simple. Let's look at an example in Ruby; let's assume that we currently have `secret_api_token` defined in our application's code:

```
secret_api_token = '123abc'
```

We can remove the token and replace it with an environment variable:

```
secret_api_token = ENV['SECRET_TOKEN']
```

In addition to protecting our credentials, using environment variables makes our application more configurable. We'll be able to quickly make configuration changes without having to change code and redeploy.

 The terms "configuration variable" and "environment variable" are interchangeable. Heroku usually uses "configuration" due to how tightly the variables are coupled with the state of the application.

How to do it...

Heroku makes it easy to set our application's environment variables through the `config` command. Let's launch a terminal and navigate to an existing Heroku project to try it out, using the following steps:

1. We can use the `config` command to see a list of all our existing environment variables:

   ```
   $ heroku config
   ```

2. To view only the value of a specific variable, we can use `get`:

   ```
   $ heroku config:get DATABASE_URL
   ```

3. To set a new variable, we can use `set`:

   ```
   $ heroku config:set VAR_NAME=var_value
   Setting config vars and restarting load-tester-rails... done, v28
   VAR_NAME: var_value
   ```

4. Each time we set a `config` variable, Heroku will restart our application. We can set multiple values at once to avoid multiple restarts:

   ```
   $ heroku config:set SECRET=value SECRET2=value
   Setting config vars and restarting load-tester-rails... done, v29
   SECRET:  value
   SECRET2: value
   ```

5. To delete a variable, we use `unset`:

   ```
   $ heroku config:unset SECRET
   Unsetting SECRET and restarting load-tester-rails... done, v30
   ```

6. If we want, we can delete multiple variables with a single command:

   ```
   $ heroku config:unset VAR_NAME SECRET2
   Unsetting VAR_NAME and restarting load-tester-rails... done, v31
   Unsetting SECRET2 and restarting load-tester-rails... done, v32
   ```

Heroku tracks each configuration change as a release. This makes it easy for us to roll back changes if we make a mistake.

How it works...

Environment variables are used on Unix-based operating systems to manage and share configuration information between applications. As they are so common, changing our application to use them does not lock us into deploying only to Heroku.

Heroku stores all of our configuration variables in one central location. Each change to these variables is tracked, and we can view the history by looking through our past releases. When Heroku spins up a new dyno, part of the process is taking all of our configuration settings and setting them as environment variables on the dyno. This is why whenever we make a configuration change, Heroku restarts our dynos.

 As configuration variables are such a key part of our Heroku application, any change to them will also be included in our Heroku logs.

See also

▸ Read about the Twelve-Factor app's rule on configuration at `http://12factor.net/config`

Enabling the maintenance page

Occasionally, we will need to make changes to our application that requires downtime. The proper way to do this is to put up a maintenance page that displays a friendly message and respond to all the incoming HTTP requests with a `503 Service Unavailable` status.

Doing this will keep our users informed and also avoid any negative SEO effects. Search engines understand that when they receive a 503 response, they should come back later to recrawl the site. If we didn't use a maintenance page and our application returned a 404 or 500 error instead, it's possible that a search engine crawler might remove the page from their index.

How to do it...

Let's open up a terminal and navigate to one of our Heroku projects to begin with, using the following steps:

1. We can view if our application's maintenance page is currently enabled with the `maintenance` command:

   ```
   $ heroku maintenance

     off
   ```

2. Let's try turning it on. This will stop traffic from being routed to our dynos and show the maintenance page as follows:

   ```
   $ heroku maintenance:on

   Enabling maintenance mode for load-tester-rails... done
   ```

3. Now, if we visit our application, we'll see the default Heroku maintenance page:

Application Offline for Maintenance

This application is undergoing maintenance right now. Please check back later.

---

4. To disable the maintenance page and resume sending users to our application, we can use the `maintenance:off` command:

   ```
   $ heroku maintenance:off

   Disabling maintenance mode for load-tester-rails... done
   ```

See also

▶ To learn how to customize the maintenance page, take a look at *Chapter 4, Production-ready with Heroku*

Managing releases and rolling back

What do we do if disaster strikes and our newly released code breaks our application? Luckily for us, Heroku keeps a copy of every deploy and configuration change to our application. This enables us to roll back to a previous version while we work to correct the errors in our latest release.

 Heads up! Rolling back only affects application code and configuration variables. Add-ons and our database will not be affected by a rollback.

In this recipe, we will learn how to manage our releases and roll back code from the CLI.

How to do it...

In this recipe, we'll view and manage our releases from the Heroku CLI, using the `releases` command. Let's open up a terminal now and navigate to one of our Heroku projects by performing the following steps:

1. Heroku tracks every deploy and configuration change as a release. We can view all of our releases from both the CLI and the web dashboard with the `releases` command:

   ```
   $ heroku releases

   === load-tester-rails Releases

   v33  Add WEB_CON config vars  coutermarsh.mike@gmail.com
   2014/03/30 11:18:49 (~ 5h ago)

   v32  Remove SEC config vars        coutermarsh.mike@gmail.com
   2014/03/29 19:38:06 (~ 21h ago)

   v31  Remove VAR config vars        coutermarsh.mike@gmail.com
   2014/03/29 19:38:05 (~ 21h ago)

   v30  Remove  config vars        coutermarsh.mike@gmail.com
   2014/03/29 19:27:05 (~ 21h ago)

   v29  Deploy 9218c1c vars  coutermarsh.mike@gmail.com  2014/03/29
   19:24:29 (~ 21h ago)
   ```

2. Alternatively, we can view our releases through the Heroku dashboard. Visit `https://dashboard.heroku.com`, select one of our applications, and click on **Activity**:

3. We can view detailed information about each release using the `info` command. This shows us everything about the change and state of the application during this release:

```
$ heroku releases:info v33

=== Release v33

Addons: librato:development
        newrelic:stark
        rollbar:free
        sendgrid:starter


By:     coutermarsh.mike@gmail.com
Change: Add WEB_CONCURRENCY config vars
When:   2014/03/30 11:18:49 (~ 6h ago)


=== v33 Config Vars
WEB_CONCURRENCY: 3
```

4. We can revert to the previous version of our application with the `rollback` command:

```
$ heroku rollback

Rolling back load-tester-rails... done, v32

  !    Warning: rollback affects code and config vars; it doesn't
add or remove addons. To undo, run: heroku rollback v33
```

Rolling back creates a new version of our application in the release history.

5. We can also specify a specific version to roll back to:

```
$ heroku rollback v30

Rolling back load-tester-rails... done, v30
```

The version we roll back to does not have to be an older version. Although it sounds contradictory, we can also roll back to newer versions of our application.

How it works...

Behind the scenes, each Heroku release is tied to a specific slug and set of configuration variables. As Heroku keeps a copy of each slug that we deploy, we're able to quickly roll back to previous versions of our code without having to rebuild our application.

For each deploy release created, it will include a reference to the git SHA that was pushed to master. The git SHA is a reference to the last commit made to our repository before it was deployed. This is useful if we want to know exactly what code was pushed out in that release.

On our local machine, we can run the `$ git checkout git-sha-here` command to view our application's code in the exact state it was when deployed.

Running one-off tasks and dynos

In more traditional hosting environments, developers will often log in to servers to perform basic administrative tasks or debug an issue. With Heroku, we can do this by launching one-off dynos. These are dynos that contain our application code but do not serve web requests.

For a Ruby on Rails application, one-off dynos are often used to run database migrations or launch a Rails console.

How to do it...

In this recipe, we will learn how to execute commands on our Heroku applications with the `heroku run` command. Let's launch a terminal now to get started with the following steps:

1. To have Heroku start a one-off dyno and execute any single command, we will use `heroku run`. Here, we can try it out by running a simple command to print some text to the screen:

    ```
    $ heroku run echo "hello heroku"

      Running `echo "hello heroku"` attached to terminal... up,
    run.7702

      "hello heroku"
    ```

     One-off dynos are automatically shut down after the command has finished running.

2. We can see that Heroku is running this command on a dyno with our application's code. Let's run `ls` to see a listing of the files on the dyno. They should look familiar:

    ```
    $ heroku run ls

      Running `ls` attached to terminal... up, run.5518

      app  bin  config  config.ru  db  Gemfile  Gemfile.lock  lib  log
    Procfile    public  Rakefile  README  README.md  tmp
    ```

3. If we want to run multiple commands, we can start up a bash session. Type `exit` to close the session:

    ```
    $ heroku run bash

    Running `bash` attached to terminal... up, run.2331

    ~ $ ls

    app  bin  config  config.ru  db  Gemfile  Gemfile.lock        lib
    log  Procfile  public  Rakefile  README  README.md  tmp

    ~ $ echo "hello"

    hello

    ~ $ exit

    exit
    ```

4. We can run tasks in the background using the `detached` mode. The output of the command goes to our logs rather than the screen:

    ```
    $ heroku run:detached echo "hello heroku"
    Running `echo hello heroku` detached... up, run.4534
    Use `heroku logs -p run.4534` to view the output.
    ```

5. If we need more power, we can adjust the size of the one-off dynos. This command will launch a bash session in a 2X dyno:

    ```
    $ heroku run --size=2X bash
    ```

6. If we are running one-off dynos in the detached mode, we can view their status and stop them in the same way we would stop any other dyno:

    ```
    $ heroku ps
    === run: one-off processes
    run.5927 (1X): starting 2014/03/29 16:18:59 (~ 6s ago)
    $ heroku ps:stop run.5927
    ```

How it works...

When we issue the `heroku run` command, Heroku spins up a new dyno with our latest slug and runs the command. Heroku does not start our application; the only command that runs is the command that we explicitly pass to it.

One-off dynos act a little differently than standard dynos. If we create one dyno in the detached mode, it will run until we stop it manually, or it will shut down automatically after 24 hours. It will not restart like a normal dyno will.

If we run bash from a one-off dyno, it will run until we close the connection or we reach an hour of inactivity.

Managing SSH keys

Heroku manages access to our application's Git repository with SSH keys. When we first set up the Heroku Toolbelt, we had to upload either a new or existing public key to Heroku's servers. This key allows us to access our Heroku Git repositories without entering our password each time.

If we ever want to deploy our Heroku applications from another computer, we'll either need to have the same key on that computer or provide Heroku with an additional one. It's easy enough to do this via the CLI, which we'll learn in this recipe.

How to do it...

To get started, let's fire up a terminal. We'll be using the `keys` command in this recipe by performing the following steps:

1. First, let's view all of the existing keys in our Heroku account:

   ```
   $ heroku keys
   === coutermarsh.mike@gmail.com Keys
   ssh-rsa AAAAB3NzaC...46hEzt1Q== coutermarsh.mike@gmail.com
   ssh-rsa AAAAB3NzaC...6EU7Qr3S/v coutermarsh.mike@gmail.com
   ssh-rsa AAAAB3NzaC...bqCJkM4w== coutermarsh.mike@gmail.com
   ```

2. To remove an existing key, we can use `keys:remove`. To the command, we need to pass a string that matches one of the keys:

   ```
   $ heroku keys:remove "7Qr3S/v coutermarsh.mike@gmail.com"
   Removing 7Qr3S/v coutermarsh.mike@gmail.com SSH key... done
   ```

3. To add our current user's public key, we can use `keys:add`. This will look on our machine for a public key (`~/.ssh/id_rsa.pub`) and upload it:

   ```
   $ heroku keys:add
   Found existing public key: /Users/mike/.ssh/id_rsa.pub
   Uploading SSH public key /Users/mike/.ssh/id_rsa.pub... done
   ```

   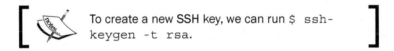

   To create a new SSH key, we can run `$ ssh-keygen -t rsa`.

4. If we'd like, we can also specify where the key is located if it is not in the default `/.ssh/` directory:

   ```
   $ heroku keys:add /path/to/key.pub
   ```

How it works...

SSH keys are the standard method for password-less authentication. There are two parts to each SSH key. There is a private key, which stays on our machine and should never be shared, and there is a public key, which we can freely upload and share.

Each key has its purpose. The public key is used to encrypt messages. The private key is used to decrypt messages.

When we try to connect to our Git repositories, Heroku's server uses our public key to create an encrypted message that can only be decrypted by our private key. The server then sends the message to our machine; our machine's SSH client decrypts it and sends the response to the server. Sending the correct response successfully authenticates us.

 SSH keys are not used for authentication to the Heroku CLI. The CLI uses an authentication token that is stored in our `~/.netrc` file.

Sharing and collaboration

We can invite collaborators through both the web dashboard and the CLI. In this recipe, we'll learn how to quickly invite collaborators through the CLI.

How to do it...

To start, let's open a terminal and navigate to the Heroku application that we would like to share, using the following steps:

1. To see the current users who have access to our application, we can use the `sharing` command:

    ```
    $ heroku sharing

    === load-tester-rails Access List

    coutermarsh.mike@gmail.com    owner

    mike@form26.com               collaborator
    ```

2. To invite a collaborator, we can use `sharing:add`:

    ```
    $ heroku sharing:add coutermarshmike@gmail.com

    Adding coutermarshmike@gmail.com to load-tester-rails as
    collaborator... done
    ```

     Heroku will send an e-mail to the user we're inviting, even if they do not already have a Heroku account.

3. If we'd like to revoke access to our application, we can do so with `sharing:remove`:

    ```
    $ heroku sharing:remove coutermarshmike@gmail.com

    Removing coutermarshmike@gmail.com from load-tester-rails
    collaborators... done
    ```

How it works...

When we add another collaborator to our Heroku application, they are granted the same abilities as us, except that they cannot manage paid add-ons or delete the application. Otherwise, they have full control to administrate the application. If they have an existing Heroku account, their SSH key will be immediately added to the application's Git repository.

See also

> ▶ Interested in using multiple Heroku accounts on a single machine? Take a look at the Heroku-accounts plugin at `https://github.com/ddollar/heroku-accounts`.

Monitoring load average and memory usage

We can monitor the resource usage of our dynos from the command line using the `log-runtime-metrics` plugin. This will give us visibility into the CPU and memory usage of our dynos. With this data, we'll be able to determine if our dynos are correctly sized, detect problems earlier, and determine whether we need to scale our application.

How to do it...

Let's open up a terminal; we'll be completing this recipe with the CLI by performing the following steps:

1. First, we'll need to install the `log-runtime-metrics` plugin via the CLI. We can do this easily through `heroku labs`:

   ```
   $ heroku labs:enable log-runtime-metrics
   ```

2. Now that the runtime metrics plugin is installed, we'll need to restart our dynos for it to take effect:

   ```
   $ heroku restart
   ```

3. Now that the plugin is installed and running, our dynos' resource usage will be printed to our logs. Let's view them now:

   ```
   $ heroku logs

   heroku[web.1]: source=web.1 dyno=heroku.21 sample#load_avg_1m=0.00
   sample#load_avg_5m=0.00

   heroku[web.1]: source=web.1 dyno=heroku.21 sample#memory_
   total=105.28MB sample#memory_rss=105.28MB sample#memory_
   cache=0.00MB sample#memory_swap=0.00MB sample#memory_
   pgpgin=31927pages sample#memory_pgpgout=4975pages
   ```

4. From the logs, we can see that for this application, our load average is 0, and this dyno is using a total of 105 MB of RAM.

How it works...

Now that we have some insight into how our dynos are using resources, we need to learn how to interpret these numbers. Understanding the utilization of our dynos will be key for us if we ever need to diagnose a performance-related issue.

In our logs, we will now see `load_avg_1m` and `load_avg_5m`. This is our dynos' load average over a 1-minute and 5-minute period. The timeframes are helpful in determining whether we're experiencing a brief spike in activity or it is more sustained. Load average is the amount of total computational work that the CPU has to complete. The 1X and 2X dynos have access to four virtual cores. A load average of four means that the dynos' CPU is fully utilized. Any value above four is a warning sign that the dyno might be overloaded, and response times could begin to suffer. Web applications are typically not CPU-intensive applications, so seeing low load averages for web dynos should be expected. If we start seeing high load averages, we should consider either adding more dynos or using larger dynos to handle the load.

Our memory usage is also shown in the logs. The key value that we want to keep track of is `memory_rrs`, which is the total amount of RAM being utilized by our application. It's best to keep this value no higher than 50 to 70 percent of the total RAM available on the dyno. For a 1X dyno with 512 MB of memory, this would mean keeping our memory usage no greater than 250 to 350 MB. This allows our application room to grow under load and helps us avoid any memory swapping. Seeing values above 70 percent is an indication that we need to either adjust our application's memory usage or scale up.

Memory swap occurs when our dyno runs out of RAM. To compensate, our dyno will begin using its hard drive to store data that will normally be stored in RAM. For any web application, any swap should be considered evil. This value should always be zero. If our dyno starts swapping, we can expect that it will significantly slow down our application's response times. Seeing any swap is an immediate indication that we must either reduce our application's memory consumption or start scaling.

See also

▶ Load average and memory usage are particularly useful when performing application load tests. Take a look at *Chapter 6, Load Testing a Heroku Application* to learn more.

3
Setting Up a Staging Environment

In this chapter, we will cover:

- ▶ Duplicating an existing application
- ▶ Managing git remotes
- ▶ Password protection for a Rails app
- ▶ Deploying with Heroku labs—Pipeline
- ▶ Deploying from tags
- ▶ Continuous integration and deployment with Travis CI

Introduction

Before releasing our latest code into the world, it's critical to have a staging environment that mimics our production application. This allows us to deploy code and catch issues internally before our users are affected. We want this staging environment to be exactly the same or very close to what is in production. Problems that come up with our application at this stage are often related to incorrect configuration or issues with Heroku itself. If our production and staging environments are the same in configuration, any issue that would occur in production will also be seen in staging. In this chapter, we will cover everything we need to know to set up a staging environment for our application.

Duplicating an existing application

We can make an exact copy of our current application using the `heroku fork` command. This copies our application code, add-ons, databases, and configuration variables over to another application. If all of our application's third-party services are Heroku add-ons, creating a fork would cover everything we need to do to get another environment up and running quickly.

How to do it...

Let's get started by opening up a terminal and navigating to the Heroku application that we'd like to fork. We'll create our forked application using the CLI by performing the following steps:

1. To fork the current directories' application, we will use the `fork` command along with our new application's name:

    ```
    $ heroku fork new-applications-name
    Creating fork new-applications-name... done
    Copying slug... done
    Adding librato:development... done
    Adding newrelic:stark... done
    Adding rollbar:free... done
    Adding sendgrid:starter... done
    Adding heroku-postgresql:dev... done
    Adding pgbackups:plus to load-tester-rails... done
    Adding pgbackups:plus to staging-load-testing... done
    Transferring database (this can take some time)...  done
    Adding heroku-postgresql:hobby-dev... done
    Transferring database (this can take some time)...  done
    Copying config vars... done
    Fork complete.
    ```

     This process will copy over our existing database if we have one. If our database has a lot of data, the process can be lengthy.

2. We can also specify the name of the application we want to fork. This is useful if we're not currently in the application's directory:

    ```
    $ heroku fork -a original-application-name new-applications-name
    ```

3. The final option available to us is forking into another Heroku region. If our current application is in the US region, we can create a version in Europe using the following command:

```
$ heroku fork new-applications-name—region eu
```

 The region can be either us or eu. Note that they are lowercase.

How it works...

Forking an application involves copying over the parent application's slug, add-ons, configuration variables, and database.

Add-ons

Each add-on that was on the parent application will be recreated on the forked application using the same plan. If our forked application doesn't necessarily need the same level of add-ons as the parent, we must ensure that we downgrade them after forking to avoid any unnecessary charges.

Config variables

Heroku copies over all of our existing configuration variables with the exception of add-on-specific variables (such as our database credentials). If we use any third-party services that are outside Heroku's add-ons, we'll need to adjust their configuration settings manually.

Database

As long as we are using Heroku Postgres, a new database will be created during the fork process. All of the data in our parent database will also be copied over. The amount of time this takes will depend on the size of our database. If we are using a third-party database, we'll have to do this manually on our own.

See also

▶ To learn more about the Heroku fork, take a look at the documentation available at https://devcenter.heroku.com/articles/fork-app

Managing git remotes

Once we have multiple environments on Heroku for our application, we will need to learn how to push the same application code up to each different environment. This can be easily accomplished by adding additional git remotes on our machine. A Git remote is the location where Git pushes code to from our local machine. We can set up as many remotes as we like. It's common to have remotes for production, staging, and origin (most likely, GitHub or BitBucket).

When we push code to Heroku, the command typically looks like this:

```
$ git push heroku master
```

The name of the git remote that we're pushing to is heroku. We can change the name and destination of our remotes to anything we want. By default, Heroku sets up a remote named "heroku" for our application. In this recipe, you will learn how to add additional remotes so that you can push the same code to multiple Heroku applications.

How to do it...

First, we'll want to see what our current git remotes are. So, let's open a terminal and navigate to one of our Heroku projects by performing the following steps:

1. Let's look at our existing remotes by running the git remote command with the -v flag. This gives us the verbose listing of our remotes, showing us exactly where our code can be pushed:

   ```
   $ git remote -v
   heroku git@heroku.com:load-tester-rails.git (fetch)
   heroku git@heroku.com:load-tester-rails.git (push)
   origin
     https://github.com/mscoutermarsh/rails_load_test_heroku.git
   (fetch)
   origin
     https://github.com/mscoutermarsh/rails_load_test_heroku.git
   (push)
   ```

   Here, we can see that we currently have two remotes: heroku and origin. In this case, origin is pointing to a repository on GitHub, and heroku is pointing to our application running on Heroku.

There is a listing for both `fetch` and `push`. In this example, they are the same. Git gives us the flexibility to pull (fetch) code from a different repository than the one we push it to. This is not something that we will be using here, but it is good to be aware of it.

2. Next, let's set up another git remote for our staging application. This will allow us to easily deploy our code to the staging application. Heroku makes this easy with the `git:remote` command. Let's try it now:

    ```
    $ heroku git:remote—app staging-load-testing—remote staging
    Git remote staging added
    ```

3. If we take a look at our git remotes again, we will see our new staging remote:

    ```
    $ git remote -v
    heroku git@heroku.com:load-tester-rails.git (fetch)
    heroku git@heroku.com:load-tester-rails.git (push)
    origin
      https://github.com/mscoutermarsh/rails_load_test_heroku.git
    (fetch)
    origin
      https://github.com/mscoutermarsh/rails_load_test_heroku.git
    (push)
    staging git@heroku.com:staging-load-testing.git (fetch)
    staging git@heroku.com:staging-load-testing.git (push)
    ```

4. We can now easily deploy code to our staging environment. We simply need to use our new remote's name in the `git push` command:

    ```
    $ git push staging master
    ```

     To remove a remote, we can use `$ git remote remove name_of_remote`.

How it works...

Being able to push to and pull from remotes is the core piece of Git that allows us to collaborate with others by sharing our changes. Remote repositories are alternate versions of our repository hosted somewhere on the Internet. We are probably most used to seeing remotes hosted on services such as GitHub or BitBucket.

Password protection for a Rails app

Once we deploy our staging application and it's accessible on the Internet, we'll want to restrict access to it. This will protect us from any users accidently coming across it or search engines crawling and indexing it.

In this recipe, we will learn how to add basic HTTP authentication to a Rails application.

Getting ready

For this recipe, we'll need an existing Rails application to modify. If we don't have one, we can use the application that we set up in *Chapter 1, Getting Started with Heroku*.

How to do it...

Every Rails application has a configuration file specific to each environment that it runs in. Each of these config files can be found in the `config/environments` folder. Let's perform the following steps:

1. To start, we'll want to create a new environment file for staging. Let's do this now by creating a `staging.rb` file in the `config/environments` folder.

2. In this file, we'll add the following code:

```
# Based on production defaults
require Rails.root.join('config/environments/production')
ApplicationNameHere::Application.configure do
config.middleware.use '::Rack::Auth::Basic' do |user, password|
[user, password] == ['staging', ENV['STAGING_PASS']]
  end
end
```

 Replace `ApplicationNameHere` in line 3 with your application's name.

3. That's it for code changes. Let's commit our new staging configuration to Git and push it up to Heroku:

```
$ git add .
$ git commit -m 'Setting up staging environment file'
$ git push staging master
```

4. Our authentication method retrieves our staging password from an environment variable. Let's set this now for our staging application:

```
$ heroku config:set STAGING_PASS=top_secret RAILS_ENV=staging-app
staging-application-name
```

5. For Rails to know that we want to use the staging configuration, we have to set our `RAILS_ENV` variable to staging. We can do this with a configuration variable as well:

```
$ heroku config:set RAILS_ENV=staging-app staging-application-name
```

6. We're now ready to test out our new password protection. Let's launch our app and take a look at it:

```
$ heroku open
```

The following screenshot appears when the preceding command is run:

How it works...

In this recipe, we used the Rack middleware to add basic HTTP authentication to our Rails application. Rack is a lightweight piece of software that handles the sending and receiving of web requests. It sits directly between our web server and the Rails framework, facilitating the messages between Rails and whichever web server we are using. Rack has add-ons known as middleware. It's easiest to think of middleware as a filter placed inside Rack. All web requests pass through the middleware on both their way in and out of our application. In this recipe, we used the `Rack::Auth::Basic` middleware to secure our staging environment. It checks each request and verifies that the user has provided the correct credentials before it allows the request through.

Basic authentication works with all browsers. After logging in once, our browser will store the credentials and continue to send them with each request to the application.

See also

▶ The source code for `Rack::Auth::Basic` is available on GitHub at `https://github.com/rack/rack/blob/master/lib/rack/auth/basic.rb`

Deploying with Heroku labs – Pipeline

Each time we deploy our code to Heroku, a new slug is created; this slug contains all of our application code and assets. Using Heroku's Pipeline, we can promote this slug to another environment without having to go through the slug-compilation process again. This ensures that the slug that we tested and verified in our staging environment is identical to what we push to our production environment. With the Pipeline, we can compare the commits between our applications so that we know exactly what changes we are deploying. It's amazingly useful; here, we will learn how to set it up and use it.

How to do it...

To get started, let's open up a terminal and navigate to our Heroku project by performing the following steps:

1. First, we need to install the Heroku Pipeline CLI plugin:

    ```
    $ heroku plugins:install git@github.com:heroku/heroku-pipeline.git
    Installing heroku-pipeline... done
    ```

 Heroku Pipeline's GitHub repository at `https://github.com/heroku/heroku-pipeline` is a great resource for more information.

2. Now that it's installed, we'll need to enable it for our Heroku application:

    ```
    $ heroku labs:enable pipelines
    Enabling pipelines for coutermarsh.mike@gmail.com... done
    WARNING: This feature is experimental and may change or be removed
    without notice.
    For more information see: https://devcenter.heroku.com/articles/
    using-pipelines-to-deploy-between-applications
    ```

3. Let's check the status of our staging pipeline. To do this, we'll use the `pipeline` command:

```
$ heroku pipeline—app staging-application-name

!    Downstream app not specified. Use `heroku pipeline:add
DOWNSTREAM_APP` to add one.
```

4. Next, we need to tell Heroku which application is our `downstream` app. This is the application that we want our slug to go to next. Let's set our staging application's downstream to our production application:

```
$ heroku pipeline:add production-application-name—app staging-
application-name

Added downstream app: production-application-name
```

5. Let's run the `pipeline` command again, just to verify that it worked and everything is set up correctly:

```
$ heroku pipeline—app staging-application-name

'Pipeline: staging-application-name ---> production-application-
name'
```

6. We can compare the code between our staging (upstream) and production (downstream) applications. This will show each commit that is different between the two environments. This is very useful to know exactly what we are about to deploy:

```
$ heroku pipeline:diff—app staging-application-name

Comparing staging-application-name to production-application-
name...done, staging-application-name ahead by 1 commit:

bf82537  2014-04-18  a test commit   (Mike Coutermarsh)
```

7. Now that we've compared the commits between the two applications, let's try to promote our staging slug to production:

```
$ heroku pipeline:promote—app staging-application-name

Promoting staging-application-name to production-application-
name.....done, v41
```

8. That's it! Our staging slug has been promoted and is now in production. We can verify that this worked by checking the releases for our production application:

```
$ heroku releases—app production-application-name

=== production-application-name Releases

v41  Promote staging-application-name v15 bf82537   coutermarsh.
mike@gmail.com  2014/04/19 13:02:33 (~ 2m ago)
```

How it works...

Behind the scenes, the pipeline plugin is a small Ruby application that uses the Cisaurus API, also known as **CI-as-a-service Heroku API**. It keeps track of our application's downstream for us, and once we run the `promote` command, it sends a request to the Cisaurus API, telling it to copy the slug from our current application to the downstream application.

The pipeline plugin is useful for more than just moving slugs from staging to production. We can get much more complex by having multiple environments that our code progresses through. Developers can even have their own independent testing environment that uses the staging environment as a downstream.

 The pipeline will not automatically run any data migrations for us. We have to do this manually in the same way as a normal deploy.

See also

▶ To learn more, Pipeline's source code is available on GitHub at `https://github.com/heroku/heroku-pipeline`

Deploying from tags

Git tags are an easy way to track the versions of our application. In this recipe, we'll learn how to tag our Git repositories and then deploy specific versions to Heroku.

How to do it...

To start, let's open up a terminal and navigate to one of our Heroku apps by performing the following steps:

1. We can add our first tag with the `git tag` command. We'll need to specify the tag as well as a message that describes it:

   ```
   $ git tag -a v1.0 -m "Version 1 release. Example of a release tag"
   ```

    The tag does not have to be a version number. We can use anything we want.

2. Next, we'll want to push our new tag up to our origin repository:

```
$ git push—tags origin
Counting objects: 1, done.
Writing objects: 100% (1/1), 187 bytes | 0 bytes/s, done.
Total 1 (delta 0), reused 0 (delta 0)
To https://github.com/mscoutermarsh/refinery_heroku.git
* [new tag]          v1.0 -> v1.0
```

3. If we're using GitHub to host our repository, we will now see a new tag under the **Releases** section.

4. The last step is to push the tag to Heroku. We can do this with the following command:

```
$ git push -f heroku v1.0^{}:master
```

How it works...

The `push` command we used in this recipe looks a little different than the one we are used to. Let's break down exactly what happened in the preceding example. In the command, `v1.0` is the name of the tag that we previously created. The `^{}` symbol after the tag is a Git shorthand that tells Git we want to push the git commit that corresponds to the `v1.0` tag. The final part of the command, `:master`, tells Git to push to the tag as the master branch. We do this because Heroku only deploys from the master branch.

 We can run `git tag list` to see all the tags of our repositories.

See also

▸ There is a great gem called **Paratrooper** that can be used to customize the tagging and push processes to Heroku. It's great for more advanced use cases. Check it out at `https://github.com/mattpolito/paratrooper`.

Continuous integration and deployment with Travis CI

Travis CI is a service that will automatically run our application's test suite for us after we push each commit to GitHub. This gives us a reliable and repeatable process to test our code continuously.

We can take Travis CI a step further and have it deploy our code after each successful build. This allows us to focus our time on writing code rather than deploying it. The entire test and the deploy process is automated for us, as shown in the following diagram:

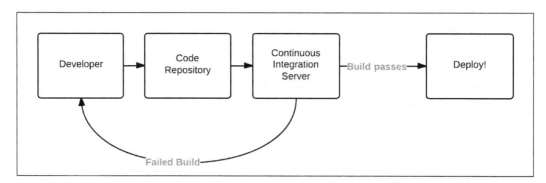

The process begins with the **Continuous Integration** (**CI**) server and ends with the latest code being deployed to either a staging or production environment. The CI server is where the latest version of our code is built and its automated test suite is run. If the build on the CI server passes (goes green), we will move on to the next step of automatically deploying the code. If the build fails, the developer is alerted, fixes the code, and starts the process again.

This process works well with the general Heroku philosophy. We automate as much as possible, making life easy for the developer.

For this recipe, you'll need to be using GitHub as your Git repository host. If you do not have an existing project set up on GitHub, feel free to use the Refinery Rails application that we set up in *Chapter 1, Getting Started with Heroku*. You can fork the source code to your own GitHub account from `https://github.com/mscoutermarsh/refinery_heroku/fork`.

Getting ready

Travis CI is one of the most popular Continuous Integration services. It's completely free for open source projects; they also have paid plans for private repositories.

Before we start using Travis, we'll need to sign up for it and enable it for our GitHub repository. If our repository is public, we'll use `https://travis-ci.org/`. If it is private, we'll need to use `https://travis-ci.com/`. The directions for each are the same and are explained as follows:

1. Let's head over to `https://travis-ci.org/` (or `.com` for private repositories) and sign up using our GitHub account. This will allow Travis to access our repositories. It will need access to pull our code and run our tests after each commit.

2. Once signed up, we'll need to visit our profile page at `https://travis-ci.org/profile`. We'll see a list of our repositories. Let's click on the toggle next to the repository we want to build; this will enable it and set up the webhooks to trigger builds in the future.

> Want to learn more? Details on how to get started with Travis are available at `http://docs.travis-ci.com/user/getting-started/` for each supported language.

How to do it...

We're now ready to start continuously testing and deploying our code. To begin with, let's open up a terminal by performing the following steps:

1. We'll use the Travis gem in this recipe. Let's install it now:

```
$ gem install travis
```

2. To deploy our application to Heroku, we need to provide Travis with a Heroku API key. We can do this by creating a Travis config file in the root directory of our application. Let's do this now with the `touch` command:

```
$ touch .travis.yml
```

> The `touch` command simply creates a blank file for us.

3. Now that we have a blank Travis file ready, let's use the Travis CLI to configure it for us to deploy to Heroku:

```
$ travis setup heroku

Detected repository as mscoutermarsh/example-app, is this correct?
|yes| yes

Heroku application name: |staging-app| staging-app

Deploy only from mscoutermarsh/example-app? |yes| yes

Encrypt API key? |yes| yes
```

 Only the Travis CI will be able to decrypt our Heroku API credentials, making them safe to store in a public GitHub repository.

4. Now, let's take a look at our `.travis.yml` file that has been set up for Heroku. We'll see our encrypted token, application name, and GitHub repository, all listed:

```
$ cat .travis.yml

deploy:
  provider: heroku
  api_key:
    secure: J8ubqQEwN0eGrN1FdXonp+79fn0OWtvC0cft123
  app: refinery-staging
  on:
    repo: github-name/repository-name
```

5. The final step in configuring Travis is telling it how to run our application's test suite. If our application uses `rspec` for testing, we will add the following line to our `.travis.yml` file:

```
deploy:
  provider: heroku
  api_key:
    secure: J8ubqQEwN0eGrN1FdXonp+79fn0OWtvC0cft123
  app: refinery-staging
  on:
    repo: github-name/repository-name
script: bundle exec rspec
```

 For a completed example, take a look at `https://github.com/mscoutermarsh/refinery_heroku/blob/travis/.travis.yml`.

6. We're now ready for Travis to build and deploy our code. Let's commit our new `.travis.yml` file and push it to GitHub:

```
$ git add .travis.yml
$ git commit -m 'Adding Travis configuration file'
$ git push origin master
```

7. GitHub will send Travis CI a webhook that notifies it that we've pushed new code to our repository; this will trigger Travis to pull our code and start a build. It will run our tests, and if they pass, it will deploy to our application on Heroku.

How it works...

Travis CI does most of the heavy lifting for us here. We simply need to correctly define the `.travis.yml` file with our Heroku account information. We can see exactly what Travis does for us behind the scenes by going to our Travis account and viewing the logs for our build. At the end of the logs, we'll have a step-by-step look at how to deploy our code. We can see that Travis uses the Heroku API and our API key to access our Heroku account and deploy it.

In this example, we set up Travis to deploy to our Heroku application (`staging-application-name`) whenever a build completes on our master branch. This is highly configurable, and we can have different branches deploy to different Heroku applications. The script line in the `.travis.yml` file tells Travis how to run our test suite. In this example, we used the Refinery-Heroku repository from *Chapter 1, Getting Started with Heroku*, as it uses `rspec`. For more specifications on how to customize the Travis configuration, you can take a look at their online documentation available at `http://docs.travis-ci.com/user/getting-started/`.

Debugging

Setting up Travis for the first time can be a little tricky for some projects. Travis keeps detailed logs in the build history that will show exactly what went wrong. These logs should always be our first stop when debugging Travis issues.

See also

▶ For an alternative to Travis CI, take a look at Codeship at `https://codeship.io/`

▶ Take a look at the Travis CLI on GitHub at `https://github.com/travis-ci/travis.rb`

4
Production-ready with Heroku

In this chapter, we will cover:

- ▶ Managing domains from the command line
- ▶ Configuring DNS with CloudFlare
- ▶ Setting up SSL with CloudFlare
- ▶ Enabling preboot for seamless deploys
- ▶ Enabling custom maintenance and error pages
- ▶ Setting up a status page
- ▶ Setting up log draining with LogEntries

Introduction

Once it's time to transition our application from development to production, there are a few steps we'll want to take to ensure that it's prepared to serve real users.

Heroku recommends the following to run any production-level application:

- ▶ Use the latest Heroku stack (Celedron Cedar)
- ▶ Have more than one dyno running for increased reliability
- ▶ If using Heroku Postgres:
  - ❑ Use a production-tier database
  - ❑ Have database backups enabled

▶ Correct DNS settings (use a CNAME record)

▶ SSL (HTTPS) to protect user information

▶ Performance monitoring

▶ Log draining

We can quickly check whether our application meets Heroku's recommendations by going to the Heroku dashboard and performing the following steps:

1. Let's open up the dashboard from `https://dashboard.heroku.com/apps`.

2. Next, we'll need to select our application.

3. Now, we can click on **Production Check** in the top-right corner to see whether the current application meets Heroku's guidelines. If our application fails in any of the steps, we'll be directed to step-by-step instructions on how to fix them:

In this chapter, we'll cover how to get this checklist to go all green. In addition to this, we will also cover some extras to ensure that our applications are prepared for real users.

Managing domains from the command line

Heroku makes it simple for us to manage our domains and subdomains from the CLI. In this recipe, we'll learn the steps to add and remove domains from the command line.

How to do it...

To start, let's open up a new terminal and navigate to one of our Heroku applications. We can add `--app application-name` to the end of any of the following commands to run them for a specific application:

1. First, let's list our application's existing domains:

    ```
    $ heroku domains
    === demo-app Domain Names
    demo2.example.org
    example.com
    ```

2. Next, let's try to add a custom domain to our application. We can do this with the `domains:add` command:

    ```
    $ heroku domains:add example-domain.com
    ```

3. We can add subdomains using the same command. Refer to the following example:

    ```
    $ heroku domains:add testing.example-domain.com
    ```

4. If we want to avoid adding subdomains one by one, we can use a wildcard:

    ```
    $ heroku domains:add *.example-domain.com
    ```

5. Removing an existing domain is simple. Let's try this now:

    ```
    $ heroku domains:remove example-domain.com
    ```

6. Finally, if we want to remove all the domains from an application, we can use `clear`:

    ```
    $ heroku domains:clear
    ```

How it works...

When Heroku receives a request at its routing layer, it knows which application to send the request to, based on the domain. By adding our domains and subdomains via the CLI, we let Heroku know how to route all the requests to our specific Heroku application.

See also

► To learn more about custom domains on Heroku, take a look at the documentation available at `https://devcenter.heroku.com/articles/custom-domains`

Configuring DNS with CloudFlare

There are many ways to point a domain name to our Heroku application. Here, we will learn how to do this using CloudFlare, a popular CDN service. CloudFlare handles our **Domain Name System** (**DNS**) for us, but it also gives us some additional benefits over a typical DNS service. As CloudFlare is a CDN, it will distribute our static assets (CSS, JS, and images) across its global network, in addition to managing our DNS records. This makes loading static assets faster for users throughout the world and reduces the requests that have to be served by Heroku. This will save us money on our Heroku bill and also help when scaling our applications. This functionality is available for free with CloudFlare; more advanced options are available to paid accounts.

Getting ready

First, we'll need to sign up for a CloudFlare account. So, let's go to `www.cloudflare.com` and sign up.

During the sign-up process, CloudFlare will guide us through the process of transferring our domain name's servers to CloudFlare. This will allow them to manage our DNS for us.

How to do it...

Now that we have a CloudFlare account, we need to adjust our DNS settings to point our domain to our Heroku application by performing the following steps:

1. To start, we'll need to go to the **Websites** section of CloudFlare to configure our DNS settings available at `https://www.cloudflare.com/my-websites`.

2. In the **Websites** section, let's click on the gear icon next to our domain name and then click on **DNS Settings**:

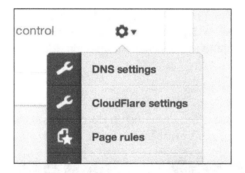

3. Here is where we will set up CloudFlare to direct visitors to our Heroku application. We will need to set up a **Canonical Name** (**CNAME**) record that points to our Heroku application's URL. Let's do this now by clicking on **Add** and then on **Save**:

4. Now that the record has been added, we can see that there is a cloud icon to the right of the record. If it's orange, it means that CloudFlare's CDN and security services are also running for this DNS record. By clicking on it, we can toggle them on and off depending on whether we want to use them or not:

5. Now, all we need to do is wait for our new DNS settings to propagate. The waiting time will depend on how long our **time to live** (**TTL**) is set to, and it can vary depending on where we are located. Once our settings take effect, we'll be able to use our domain name with our Heroku application.

How it works...

In this recipe, we used a CNAME record to point our domain to our Heroku applications. This might be a little different than what we're used to with other hosting providers. It's important for us to use a CNAME record with Heroku, because it allows us to take advantage of Heroku's DNS services as well. Our Heroku application is not served from a static IP address. At any time, it can change as Heroku moves resources around or makes changes to their network. Using a CNAME record rather than the more typical A record allows Heroku to manage these changes for us automatically.

Setting up SSL with CloudFlare

SSL (or HTTPS) is the technology that keeps all that data sent between our users and our web server safe from prying eyes. All Heroku apps already support SSL by piggybacking on Heroku's SSL certificate (`https://your-app-name.herokuapp.com`). However, unfortunately, this does not extend to any custom domains that we use for our application.

Heroku has a standard SSL add-on that we can use, but there is a simpler and more cost-effective solution—CloudFlare.

In this recipe, we'll learn how to protect our applications by enabling SSL in CloudFlare.

Getting ready

For this recipe, we'll need an existing Heroku application with a custom domain setup through CloudFlare. For step-by-step instructions on how to do this, refer to the previous recipe.

How to do it...

SSL is available on both CloudFlare's free and paid plans. If we use the free plan, we need to be aware that issuing our SSL certificate could take up to 24 hours. For a shorter turnaround time, we should upgrade to a paid plan.

 The plan information is available at `https://www.cloudflare.com/plans`.

Let's perform the following steps:

1. To start, we'll need to go to the **Websites** section of CloudFlare to configure our SSL settings: `https://www.cloudflare.com/my-websites`

2. Next to our website's name, there is a gear icon; let's click on it and go to **CloudFlare Settings**.

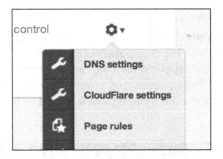

3. Now, we'll need to scroll down until we get to the SSL section of the settings page. We need to select **Full SSL (Strict)**.

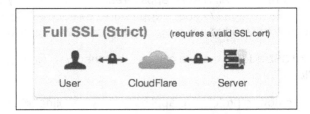

4. That's it! Now, CloudFlare will start working on issuing a new SSL certificate for us. If we're using the free plan, this might take up to 24 hours. On paid plans, it will be issued in approximately 20 minutes.

How it works...

When we turned on SSL with CloudFlare, we secured the connection between CloudFlare and our users. Conveniently, every Heroku application already has the capability to use SSL on its Heroku-provided URL (`example.herokuapp.com`). This works because Heroku allows our applications to piggyback on their SSL certificates. As our CNAME record was set to our Heroku domain, the connection between CloudFlare and Heroku was secured by the SSL that already exists for our Heroku application. The entire connection between our users and our Heroku application was secure, and we didn't have to configure a single SSL certificate!

Enabling preboot for seamless deploys

When we deploy new code to Heroku, all of our dynos are shut down and replaced with new ones simultaneously. If we have long boot times for our application, this can result in our user's requests timing out because our dynos are unable to respond to requests while booting up. We can avoid this using Heroku's preboot, a feature that gives our new dynos an additional 3 minutes to get started before shutting down our old dynos. This gives our application plenty of time to get warmed up and ready to serve requests.

How to do it...

For this recipe, we'll enable Heroku preboot from the CLI. Let's open up a terminal and navigate to a Heroku application to get started by performing the following steps:

1. First, we'll need to enable preboot for our application:

   ```
   $ heroku features:enable preboot

   Enabling preboot for example-app... done

   For more information see: https://devcenter.heroku.com/articles/
   preboot
   ```

    There must be more than one dyno running for preboot to be used. Preboot does not affect worker dynos; they will restart normally.

2. Now that preboot is enabled, we can deploy code normally, and our new dynos will be given 3 minutes to start up before traffic is directed to them, saving our users from any timeouts during the boot process:

   ```
   $ git push heroku master
   ```

How it works...

Instead of shutting down our current dynos and replacing them with new ones, Heroku boots up the new dynos first, waits for 3 minutes, and then swaps traffic over from the old dynos to the new ones. This helps us avoid any risk of requests timing out due to applications having delayed boot times. This is a more advanced feature of Heroku and does not come without risks. We should test Heroku preboot on a staging instance before using it in production. Databases and outside services will often have a maximum connection limit. During the reboot's warm-up period, we will run twice as many application instances compared to the normal period. We must be sure that our database will allow these connections simultaneously; otherwise, preboot can potentially cause more issues than it can solve.

>
> To disable Heroku preboot, we can run the `$ heroku features:disable preboot` command.

Enabling custom maintenance and error pages

Heroku has two different error pages that it will display to our users when things go wrong. The first is a general error page for when our application is unable to respond to a request. The second is the maintenance page that informs our users that our application is temporarily down and under maintenance. By default, both of these pages are very plain, and the messages they display are very general. It's easy for us to customize each of these pages and display something that we have more control over. Here, we will learn how to customize them.

>
> Here are Heroku's default error pages:
>
> ▶ **Error page**: This is available at `http://s3.amazonaws.com/heroku_pages/error.html`
>
> ▶ **Maintenance page**: This is available at `http://s3.amazonaws.com/heroku_pages/maintenance.html`

Getting ready

We need to have our error and maintenance pages hosted somewhere that's web accessible and is outside Heroku. The recommended approach is uploading them to Amazon S3; for step-by-step instructions, visit `http://docs.aws.amazon.com/AmazonS3/latest/dev/WebsiteHosting.html`.

How to do it...

In this recipe, we will use the Heroku CLI to tell Heroku where our error and maintenance pages are located. To get started, let's open up a terminal and navigate to our Heroku application by performing the following steps:

1. To set up the error page, we need to set the `ERROR_PAGE_URL` configuration variable in Heroku. Let's do this now:

    ```
    $ heroku config:set ERROR_PAGE_URL=http://example.com/my_error_
    page.html
    ```

2. Next, we'll want to set `MAINTENANCE_PAGE_URL` to the location of our maintenance page:

    ```
    $ heroku config:set MAINTENANCE_PAGE_URL=http://example.com/my_
    maintenance_page.html
    ```

3. To finish up, let's test it out by putting our application in maintenance mode and then opening our application:

    ```
    $ heroku maintenance:on
    ```

    ```
    $ heroku open
    ```

4. We should now see our new custom maintenance page displayed instead of the default Heroku one. Before we finish up, let's make sure we have re-enabled our application:

    ```
    $ heroku maintenance:off
    ```

How it works...

We can use any hosting service to serve our error page. S3 is recommended because it's very inexpensive, scalable, and highly reliable. Application-specific errors, such as 500 and 404 errors, will still be served by our application, and customizing these will depend on the framework we are using.

Setting up a status page

What will happen if our application goes down? How do we communicate with our users? The best way is to have a status page that is hosted outside Heroku. Then, if our application goes down, we can focus on fixing it rather than figuring out how to communicate with our users. Here, we will quickly learn how to set up a status page that can e-mail, SMS, or even tweet about the status of our application.

There are multiple options that can be used to build a status page with Heroku. Here, we will cover one of the most popular ones, `StatusPage.io`.

StatusPage starts at $29 per month. At the time of writing this book, there are no free options.

How to do it...

We will use the CLI to get started. Let's open up a terminal and navigate to one of our Heroku apps by performing the following steps:

1. First, let's install the add-on with `addons:add`:

   ```
   $ heroku addons:add statuspage
   ```

2. Now that it's installed, we can open up the StatusPage dashboard to configure it. It will walk us through a step-by-step process of getting our dashboard up and running. We'll be able to customize the layout, services, and record any past service outages:

   ```
   $ heroku addons:open statuspage
   ```

3. Once we complete the setup wizard, we'll have a status page that looks like what is shown in the following screenshot:

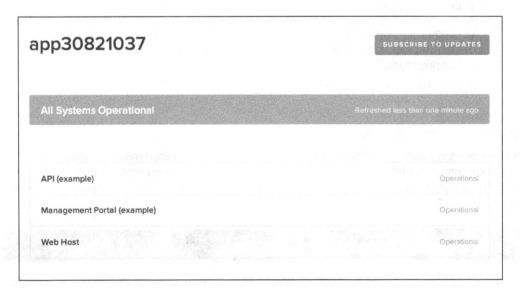

 As StatusPage integrates with Heroku, if there are any Heroku service interruptions, our page will update automatically.

4. Now that our status page is up and running, we need to learn how to report incidents. We have two options; we can either create an incident manually through the **Incidents** tab on the StatusPage dashboard, or we can use the StatusPage API.

 We can have StatusPage manage our Heroku error pages for us by clicking on **Heroku Integration** in the StatusPage dashboard.

5. Let's try creating our first incident through the API now. First, we'll need to get our StatusPage API key. We can do this by clicking on our user in the top-right corner of the dashboard, going to **Manage Account**, and then clicking on the **API** tab. On this page, we'll see both our **API key** and our **status page ID**. We'll need both to use the API.

6. Now that we have our API credentials, let's create a new incident by sending an API call with cURL. We'll need to replace the page ID and API token in the following command and then paste it into our terminal:

```
$ curl https://api.statuspage.io/v1/pages/<page ID goes here>/
incidents.json \
    -H "Authorization: OAuth <API token goes here>" \
    -X POST \
    -d "incident[name]=Database outage" \
    -d "incident[status]=identified" \
    -d "incident[wants_twitter_update]=f" \
    -d "incident[message]=We've had a hardware failure. Currently
investigating."
```

 This example is also available on GitHub at `https://gist.github.com/mscoutermarsh/1bdd27b11b3a037dce5a`.

7. Now, if we take a look at our status page, we'll see that we successfully created an incident at the top of the page:

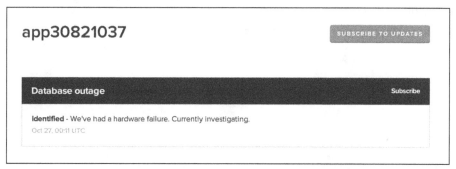

We can also have the update sent to Twitter by setting the `wants_twitter_update` parameter to `t`.

How it works...

StatusPage ties together all the information about our application's availability and displays it in one place. We can update it via the dashboard, API, or have it updated automatically by tying in third-party data sources, such as Pingdom or Librato.

See also

▶ To learn more about the StatusPage API, visit the documentation page at `http://doers.statuspage.io/api/v1/`

▶ For an alternative to StatusPage, there is StatusHub available at `https://addons.heroku.com/statushub`

Setting up log draining with LogEntries

The amount of log information that Heroku keeps for our application is limited to 1,500 lines. For a production application, this will only cover a very small span of time. We need to set up a log-draining service to keep a historical record of our logs and make it easy to search and view them. Here, we will learn how to set up Logentries on Heroku.

How to do it...

We can quickly get going with Logentries by installing it as an add-on through the CLI. Let's open up a terminal and navigate to our Heroku application to get started; then, we can perform the following steps:

1. First, let's install the Logentries add-on for our application:

```
$ heroku addons:add logentries
```

2. This command will set up a log drain that will automatically stream our logs to Logentries. Let's open it up and take a look:

```
$ heroku addons:open logentries
```

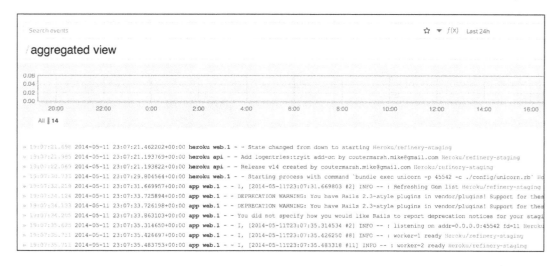

3. Logentries will automatically send us alerts when there are errors in our application. We can configure these by clicking on **Tags & Alerts** on the top navigation bar. The add-on has prepopulated most of the alerts for us.

How it works...

Heroku aggregates all of our logs in one place, known as the **Logplex**. It only keeps a brief history of our logs. It's our responsibility to record them in another service such as Logentries. Having a logging service enabled might not seem important initially. However, it's critical to have one enabled when running any production-level application. When there are issues (which there will always be), we will be thankful to have a history of exactly what happened across our application. We can also configure Logentries to alert us when there are errors in our application. Early warnings like this can help us in detecting and solving problems before they escalate into critical issues.

See also

▶ For more information on logging and the Logplex, take a look at *Chapter 2, Managing Heroku from the Command Line*

5
Error Monitoring and Logging Tools

In this chapter, we will cover:

- ► Checking Heroku's status
- ► Adjusting Rails' logging level
- ► Storing historical logs with PaperTrail
- ► Monitoring for 404 and 500 errors with PaperTrail
- ► Logging slow queries with PaperTrail
- ► Monitoring uptime with Pingdom
- ► Logging errors with Rollbar

Introduction

We can never have too much information about our application. We can prepare our application to handle as many different edge cases as possible, but our users will do the unexpected; the more monitoring we have in place, the more likely we are to find the source of problems and resolve them quickly.

In this chapter, we will learn how to set up some basic logging and monitoring services that should be enabled for any production-level application. Having high visibility into our application is essential to keep our applications performant and reliable for our users.

Checking Heroku's status

Occasionally, there will be issues with Heroku itself. The first place to look when experiencing strange issues is Heroku's status page. It keeps track of all the ongoing issues and frequently updates us with information on when we can expect them to be resolved. If we're having trouble deploying our application, seeing downtime, or just general performance issues, Heroku's status is a good place to check.

How to do it...

We can quickly check Heroku's status from the command line. Let's open up a terminal to try it out by performing the following steps:

1. We can run the following command at any time to get a quick look at Heroku's status:

    ```
    $ heroku status

    === Heroku Status

    Development: No known issues at this time.

    Production:  No known issues at this time.
    ```

2. For more detailed information, we can take a look at Heroku's status page (`https://status.heroku.com/`). It shows all the current and past service interruptions:

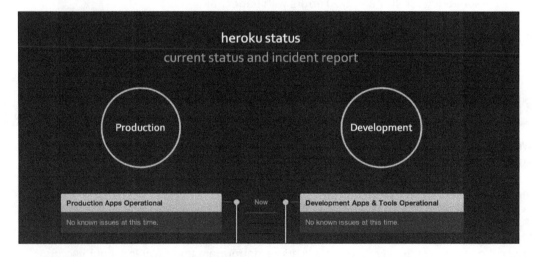

Any issues with Heroku will most likely affect our application. We can get e-mail updates for any status changes by clicking on the link in the top-right corner of the status page and subscribing to it.

How it works...

Heroku's status page splits its updates into two categories: **Production** and **Development**. Any production update can affect dynos, workers, and any production level add-ons (such as the production-tier Postgres add-ons). Development updates are specifically used for any issues with deployment, Heroku Toolbelt, or development-level database tiers.

 For updates via Twitter, follow @herokustatus.

Adjusting Rails's logging level

Heroku's Logplex will record all of our application logs that are directed to **Standard Output** (**STDOUT**). By default, Rails applications write to a logfile instead of STDOUT. Heroku solves this by automatically injecting a gem into all Rails applications to ensure that the logs are correctly recorded. This gem also gives us the ability to change our logging level on the fly using a configuration variable. In this recipe, we will learn how to adjust a Ruby on Rails application's logging level without having to redeploy any code.

Getting ready

If we do not already have a Rails application, we can use a sample application from GitHub. Open up a terminal and run the following commands to get a Rails application up and running on Heroku:

```
$ git clone https://github.com/mscoutermarsh/unicorn-rails-heroku.git
$ cd unicorn-rails-heroku
$ heroku create
$ git push heroku master
$ heroku open
```

 To commit your changes back to GitHub, you'll need to make a fork of the sample project. Learn how to fork a project at https://help.github.com/articles/fork-a-repo.

How to do it...

To start, let's open up a terminal and navigate to our Rails project. Then, we can perform the following steps:

1. We can adjust our Rails logging level by adjusting a configuration variable in Heroku. Let's run the following command to set our logging level to `debug`:

   ```
   $ heroku config:set LOG_LEVEL=debug
   ```

2. Now, Heroku will restart our app, and we can watch our logs to see the more verbose debugging output:

   ```
   $ heroku logs --tail
   ```

3. Press *Ctrl + C* to exit log viewing. Now, let's try changing our logging level again. This time, we'll set it to only display errors:

   ```
   $ heroku config:set LOG_LEVEL=error
   $ heroku logs --tail
   ```

How it works...

When deploying a Rails application to Heroku, we should always add the `rails_12factor` gem to our Gemfile. It directs our logs to STDOUT so that Heroku can record them in the Logplex. If we do not add it, Heroku will add it for us.

We can adjust our Rails logging level on the fly because the 12-factor gem injects the `rails_stdout_logging` gem into our application. This gem looks for the `LOG_LEVEL` environment variable. If it's set, it will use it for the Rails logging level.

We can set our log level to `debug`, `info`, `warn`, `error`, `fatal`, or `unknown`.

See also

> ▶ For more information on Rails log levels, take a look at the Rails documentation at `http://guides.rubyonrails.org/debugging_rails_applications.html#log-levels`

Storing historical logs with PaperTrail

Heroku only keeps the most recent 1,500 lines of logs from our application. As we scale up and add more dynos, this will only cover a very brief time period. Heroku allows us to set up log drains, which allow us to stream our logs to another service for storage. Setting up log draining is a must-have for any production application. Having our log history easily searchable will be critical when debugging our application. In this recipe, we'll learn how to set up PaperTrail to store our Heroku logs.

How to do it...

To get started, let's fire up a terminal and navigate to one of our Heroku projects. Then, we can perform the following steps:

1. First, let's add PaperTrail to our application using Heroku add-ons. The default plan is free; as our application grows, we can add more storage if necessary:

   ```
   $ heroku addons:add papertrail
   ```

 We can also install PaperTrail without going through the Heroku add-on, but then, we'd miss out on some of the enhancements that PaperTrail has made specifically for Heroku apps.

2. PaperTrail is now installed and is collecting our logs. We can open it from the command line to take a look at the dashboard:

   ```
   $ heroku addons:open papertrail
   ```

 PaperTrail will ask us if we'd like a summary of errors e-mailed to us daily. It's a good idea to subscribe to stay on top of any new problems.

3. PaperTrail sets up a few default searches that are helpful for Heroku applications. At the bottom of the screen, let's click on the icon next to the **Search** button to see what's already set up. It will filter our logs for us, showing only specific events. This becomes very useful when reading through high volumes of logs.

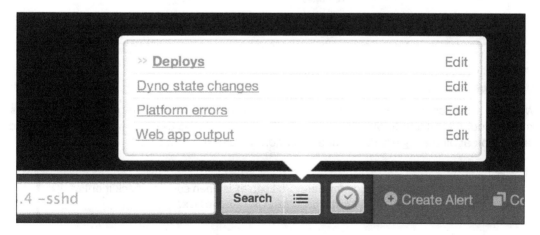

4. Let's click on the **Platform errors** filter. It will look for any Heroku error codes in our logs. This will most likely return zero results since we just set up log draining. However, now that we have run a search, we can create an alert for the search by clicking on **Create Alert** next to the search box.

5. We should set up an e-mail alert for whenever there is a Heroku error. This can notify us the minute there is an issue with our application. Let's do this now by selecting **Emails** and filling out the form. It's a good practice to have these sent out to all the developers on our team or have an e-mail list with anyone who is responsible for the application.

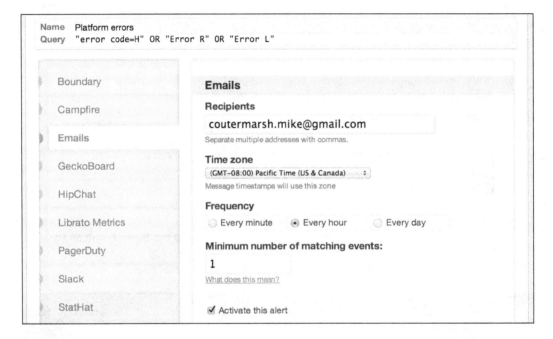

How it works...

When we provisioned the PaperTrail add-on, we added a new log drain to our application. This is an endpoint to which Heroku's Logplex will stream our logs as they are written. If we want to take a look at all the log drains of our application, we can run $ heroku drains.

 The source code for Heroku's Logplex is open source; check it out at https://github.com/heroku/logplex.

See also

> ▸ For more information on how Logplex works and logging in general, take a look at _Chapter 2, Managing Heroku from the Command Line_, and the recipes on viewing and searching logs in that chapter.

Monitoring for 404 and 500 errors with PaperTrail

We can set up various searches in PaperTrail and have it automatically e-mail a summary of all the events that match our search for the day. In this recipe, we will learn how to set up a search for specific HTTP status codes and have PaperTrail e-mail us when they are set up.

> We'll need PaperTrail set up for this recipe; refer to the previous recipe if you do not have it set up yet.

How to do it...

To start, we'll need to open up a terminal and navigate to our Heroku project with PaperTrail installed. Then, we can perform the following steps:

1. First, let's open up the PaperTrail dashboard. We can quickly do this from the command line:

    ```
    $ heroku addons:open papertrail
    ```

2. Now, we want to create a search for all the events that resulted in a 404 (Not Found) or 500 (Internal Server Error) HTTP response code. We can do this by typing `status=404 OR status=500` into the search box at the bottom of the page.

3. Next, let's click on **Search**, and we'll see the results of our query. At this point, it's fine if we do not see any errors. We want to automate this search and get the results sent to us daily. To do this, let's click on **Save Search** to the right of the search box.

4. Click on **Save & Setup an Alert** to set up automatic e-mails for this search.

5. Finally, we can set up the alert by entering our e-mail address and clicking on **1 day**. This will send us a summary of all 404s and 500s for our application daily.

How it works...

We can never have too much information about how our application is running. The more data we have, the more likely we are to catch issues before our users do. Whenever Heroku responds to a request, it includes the status code that it responds with. This makes it easy for us to filter events by status code.

Setting up daily error e-mails is a way to keep track of any increase in activity. For this search, if we see a sudden spike in 404s, we know that we probably have a dead link somewhere in our application. Taking a quick look at e-mails like this will give us an idea of the pulse of our Heroku application.

See also

► For more information on how to get the most out of the search, take a look at PaperTrail's documentation on searching available at `http://help.papertrailapp.com/kb/how-it-works/search-syntax`

Logging slow queries with PaperTrail

The first place where we'll usually experience application performance issues is in the database. A poorly written query or missing index can have a snowballing effect on our application's speed. As our application's traffic increases, detecting and fixing slow queries early on will help us avoid slow response times or even downtime.

Production-tier Heroku Postgres databases all come with logging capabilities. They are set up to send a log entry to Logplex whenever a query takes longer than 2 seconds to execute. We can use this to our advantage by setting up alerts to watch for these slow queries. In this recipe, we'll learn how to set up a search and an alert for slow queries using PaperTrail.

[This recipe will only work with production-tier Heroku Postgres databases. The hobby-tier databases do not have logging enabled.]

How to do it...

To start, let's open a terminal and navigate to our Heroku project that has the PaperTrail add-on. Then, perform the following steps:

1. First, let's open up the PaperTrail dashboard. We can do this quickly via the command line:

   ```
   $ heroku addons:open papertrail
   ```

2. Now that the dashboard is open, we'll want to create a new search for slow queries. Let's do this by typing the following into the search box:

   ```
   "app/postgres" duration
   ```

   Now, click on **Search**, and any slow queries will appear. If there aren't any, it might just mean that we haven't had any slow queries yet.

3. Next, we'll want to save this search and create an alert for it. We'll do this by clicking on **Save Search**, typing in a name for the search, and then clicking on **Save & Setup an Alert**.

4. Finally, we can set up PaperTrail to send us an e-mail when there are results that match this search. We should set the frequency of the e-mail to be daily. If our application has multiple developers, we should send it to all of them to increase the visibility of any slow queries.

How it works...

In this recipe, we took advantage of Heroku Postgres's slow query logging. Any queries that take longer than 2 seconds to complete are automatically logged for us and sent to PaperTrail via our log drain. By setting up alerts for these logs in PaperTrail, we keep ourselves informed of any database performance issues before they start to cause any serious issues.

See also

▶ Slow query alerts are just one way we can use Postgres logs. Take a look at Heroku's documentation on Postgres logging available at `https://devcenter.heroku.com/articles/postgres-logs-errors` for more ideas.

Monitoring uptime with Pingdom

To monitor our application's general speed and uptime, we need to look no further than Pingdom. Pingdom is a third-party service that sends intermittent requests to our application and measures how quickly it responds. If our application stops responding, it will send us an alert. When picking an uptime monitoring service, it's critical to choose one that is independent of the platform you're monitoring. In this case, Pingdom is not run on Heroku; this makes it a good choice to monitor Heroku applications. If Heroku is having issues, the first place we'll get an alert from is usually Pingdom.

How to do it...

It's easy to get started with Pingdom, so let's open up a browser to begin:

1. First, we'll need to sign up for an account. Let's navigate to `https://www.pingdom.com/free/` to sign up for a free account. The free account is enough for us to try out monitoring one application; we'll need to upgrade it if we want to monitor more or have additional methods of notifications.

2. Once signed up, we'll be brought to the Pingdom dashboard. In the top-right corner, let's click on **Add New** and create a monitor for our app. From here, we can adjust how often we'd like Pingdom to check our application and what to do if it does not receive a response.

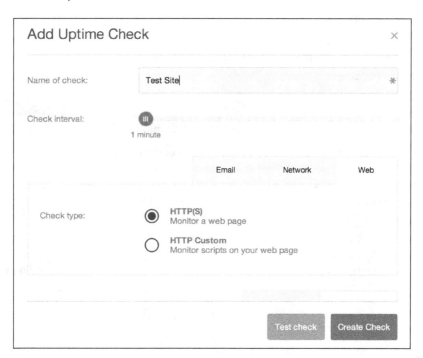

3. That's it! Pingdom will start monitoring our application and alert us of any downtime with our application.

How it works...

A `ping` is the smallest possible request to which we can get a response from a web server. We can try sending a ping from our own machine using the `ping` command. This will send a small request to `Heroku.com`, and we'll get the following response back:

```
$ ping heroku.com
PING heroku.com (50.19.85.156): 56 data bytes
64 bytes from 50.19.85.156: icmp_seq=0 ttl=40 time=30.461 ms
64 bytes from 50.19.85.156: icmp_seq=1 ttl=40 time=26.229 ms
64 bytes from 50.19.85.156: icmp_seq=2 ttl=40 time=34.493 ms
64 bytes from 50.19.85.156: icmp_seq=3 ttl=40 time=37.902 ms
64 bytes from 50.19.85.156: icmp_seq=4 ttl=40 time=35.463 ms
```

Press *Ctrl + C* to stop pinging the server.

Pingdom monitors our web application by sending these requests from different servers throughout the world. A failed response to a ping indicates that there are issues in connecting to our application, and we should investigate the failure.

See also

▶ For an alternative to Pingdom, take a look at Copper Egg available at `http://copperegg.com/`

Logging errors with Rollbar

All production applications should have some form of error logging. Whenever our application fails to serve a user's request, we'll want to know as much information as possible about the failure. Using an exception service, we can log detailed information about each error and track how frequently it occurs. Having all of this at our fingertips makes it easy to prioritize which errors to fix. In this recipe, we will learn how to install Rollbar on a Rails application.

 Rollbar supports almost every language and framework. For specific instructions on other languages, take a look at their documentation at `https://rollbar.com/docs/`.

Getting ready

You'll need a Ruby on Rails application running on Heroku to complete this recipe. If you don't have one, take a look at *Chapter 1, Getting Started with Heroku,* for instructions on how to set one up.

How to do it...

To start, let's launch a terminal and navigate to a directory with an existing Rails application. Then, perform the following steps:

1. Let's enable the Rollbar add-on via the Heroku CLI:

   ```
   $ heroku addons:add rollbar
   ----> Adding rollbar to application_name... done, v31 (free)
   ```

2. Now that Rollbar is enabled, we'll need to install it in our application. We'll need to open up our Gemfile and add the following line:

   ```
   gem 'rollbar'
   ```

3. Next, we'll run bundler to install the gem:

   ```
   $ bundle install
   ```

4. Now, let's run the Rollbar generator to set up our Rails app to report errors to Rollbar:

   ```
   $ rails generate rollbar
   ```

5. To complete installation, we'll need to commit our changes to Git and redeploy our application:

   ```
   $ git add Gemfile
   $ git add Gemfile.lock
   $ git add config/initializers/rollbar.rb
   $ git commit -m 'Adding Rollbar error logging'
   $ git push heroku master
   ```

6. Rollbar has added a testing rake task to our project to simulate an error. Let's use it now to verify that Rollbar is working:

   ```
   $ heroku run rake rollbar:test
   Reporting exception: Testing rollbar with "rake rollbar:test". If you can see this, it works.
   [Rollbar] Scheduling payload
   [Rollbar] Sending payload
   [Rollbar] Success
   ```

7. We can now open up the Rollbar dashboard. If everything is working correctly, we will see our simulated error:

```
$ heroku addons:open rollbar
```

Top 10 items in last 24 hours				view all
24hr Trend	Count 👤		Title	
┄┄┄┄┄┄┄┄┐❶	-	✖	#1 RollbarTestingException: Testing rollbar with "rake rollbar:test". If you can see this, ...	🐞
┄┄┄┄┄┄┄┄┐❶	-	✖	#2 Test error from rollbar:test	🐞

How it works...

When we install Rollbar via the Heroku add-on, it sets up an account for us and adds configuration variables to our project that store our Rollbar credentials. We can see these settings by running the following command:

```
$ heroku config
```

Rollbar is set up to intercept all of our unhandled exceptions and record the full stack trace along with any other information about the context of the error. This makes it easy for us to quickly identify and fix bugs.

Rollbar's `generate` command creates an initializer in our Rails project at `config/initializers/rollbar.rb`. This file loads Rollbar when our application starts up. Most of the file contains documentation on how to customize our installation of Rollbar. It will work without any changes, but if we want to adjust functionality, this is the place to do it.

See also

- To learn more about Rollbar, take a look at `https://rollbar.com`
- For an alternative to Rollbar, check out Bugsnag at `https://bugsnag.com/`

6
Load Testing a Heroku Application

In this chapter, we will cover:

- ▶ Monitoring dyno performance with Librato
- ▶ Monitoring application performance with New Relic
- ▶ Learning to load test with Siege
- ▶ Configuring complex load tests with Siege
- ▶ Load testing from the cloud with Blitz.io
- ▶ Testing real user scenarios with Load Impact

Introduction

We need to know how far we can push our application before it breaks, how many users it can support, how well it scales, and where the bottlenecks are.

In this chapter, we will learn how to install the monitoring tools needed to understand how our application is performing. We will then learn how to push our application to its limit by setting up and running load tests.

We will go step by step through three different methods of load testing. We'll start with the most basic test, flooding our application with HTTP requests. We'll then advance to running more complex load tests that will mimic real-life user scenarios more closely. These methods will give us the information we need to know exactly how our application will perform and what we need to improve on to handle massive amounts of traffic.

It's best to run load tests in a staging environment to avoid affecting any real users.

Monitoring dyno performance with Librato

We will need to monitor CPU and memory usage closely during load testing. Being aware of how traffic affects both will help us in determining how many dynos we need and what size dynos work best for our application. Librato provides a fantastic dashboard that allows us to monitor all of our key performance metrics. We'll see our dyno and Postgres resource usage, as well as router performance metrics. During our load tests, we'll be able to watch how many requests our application is serving and how it affects resource usage on one screen.

Librato works with any Heroku application. It does not require anything to be installed into the application itself. It gathers data by monitoring our Heroku logs and recording and graphing the data.

How to do it...

To get started, let's open up a terminal, navigate to one of our Heroku projects, and perform the following steps:

1. As Librato gathers information from our logs, we'll need to enable log runtime metrics. This plugin will print load-usage and memory-usage information straight to our Heroku logs:

   ```
   $ heroku labs:enable log-runtime-metrics
   ```

2. We'll need to restart our dynos for the change to take effect:

   ```
   $ heroku restart
   ```

3. Now, we can enable Librato and make it start collecting data for us:

   ```
   $ heroku addons:add librato
   ```

4. Let's launch the Librato dashboard and take a look at our metrics:

   ```
   $ heroku addons:open librato
   ```

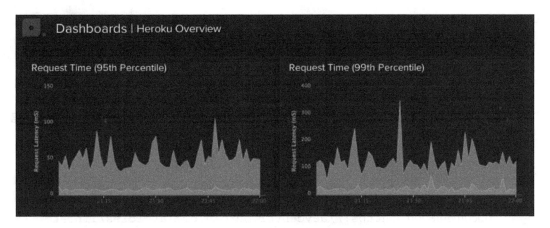

After a few minutes, we will start seeing our graphs populate with data.

 Are you not seeing any data? Make sure that the `log-runtime-metrics` plugin is installed and the application is restarted.

How it works...

Librato monitors our Heroku logs and records key pieces of data about our application. Having each metric on the same screen makes it easy for us to find a correlation between different metrics and identify the problem areas as we scale.

Some of the key terms are as follows:

- **Request time**: This indicates the total time to respond to an application request
- **Request throughput**: This indicates the number of requests served by our application per minute
- **Router queue time**: This indicates the amount of time a request spent in the Heroku routing layer before being sent to one of our web dynos
- **Dyno memory**: This indicates the average RAM and swap used by our dynos

During a load test, we will be able to see a request throughput rise and simultaneously watch the effect on our dynos' load and memory averages. Ideally, we'll see that the response times remain consistent as traffic increases. However, at a certain point, our dynos will reach their limit, and the response time will begin to suffer. During a load test, we want to be pushing our application to its limit. Under high load, the smallest problems in an application tend to reveal themselves. We do load tests so that we can uncover these issues on our own rather than having our users find them later. Tools such as Librato give us the data we need to find scaling issues in our application.

See also

▶ Librato can measure custom metrics as well. Take a look at the Heroku documentation at `https://devcenter.heroku.com/articles/librato` for more information on how to take full advantage of Librato.

Monitoring application performance with New Relic

New Relic is a must-have for any production-level web application. It has more features than can possibly be listed here. We will focus on how we can use New Relic to identify performance problems in our application. New Relic provides detailed analytics for each request our application serves. We will be able to see exactly where our application is slow and drill down into why. In this recipe, we will cover the process of installing New Relic in a Rails application. We'll then get a quick tour of the New Relic interface so that we know exactly where to look when diagnosing performance issues.

How to do it...

Before using New Relic, we'll need to install it. This will require us to add the New Relic gem to our application, as well as enable the New Relic add-on in our Heroku application.

To start, let's open a terminal and navigate to our Ruby on Rails application. If we do not have a Rails application to try this out on, we can use the example Rails application from *Chapter 1, Getting Started with Heroku*:

1. We'll need to install the New Relic add-on. Let's start out with New Relic on the free plan (`stark`):

    ```
    $ heroku addons:add newrelic:stark
    ```

To see the other available New Relic plans, visit `https://addons.heroku.com/newrelic`.

2. Now, we need to add the New Relic gem to our application's Gemfile. Let's add the following command:

```
gem 'newrelic_rpm'
```

3. Next, let's run `bundle install`:

```
$ bundle install
```

4. Now, we can commit the changes to Git and push them to Heroku:

```
$ git add Gemfile
$ git add Gemfile.lock
$ git commit -m 'adding new relic'
$ git push heroku master
```

5. We can configure some New Relic settings through environment variables. For starters, let's set our application's name and enable parameter capture:

```
$ heroku config:set NEW_RELIC_APP_NAME='Application Name'
$ heroku config:set NEW_RELIC_CAPTURE_PARAMS=TRUE
```

 Setting `NEW_RELIC_CAPTURE_PARAMS` to `true` will tell New Relic to record the parameters used in each request. Rails will filter out any sensitive parameters, such as passwords.

6. Let's open up our application and use it; this will get some data into New Relic by giving it a few requests to record:

```
$ heroku open
```

 If you are using the Refinery Rails application, remember to navigate to `/refinery`.

7. Now that we've sent some requests to our application, we can launch the New Relic dashboard and take a look at our application's data:

```
$ heroku addons:open newrelic
```

8. The first thing we'll see is a screen that shows our application's name. Let's click on it to view our data. We'll start out by seeing a high-level view of our web transactions and their response times.

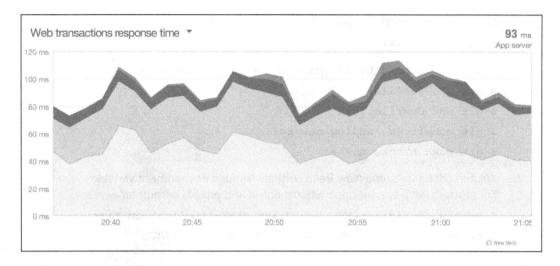

9. For the purposes of load testing, we will be most interested in digging into our application's transactions. Let's do so by clicking on **Transactions** at the top of the screen.

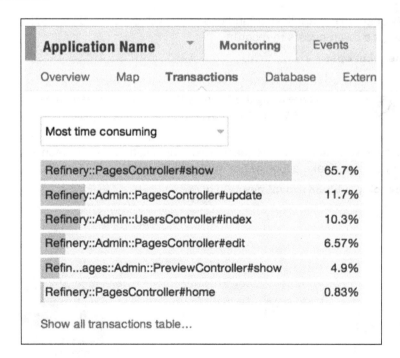

10. From this screen, we can learn which of our transactions take the most time. This is where we can determine the problem areas in our application that might need to be optimized. Let's click on one of our transactions to view more details about it.

11. Now, we will see the details about the transaction and what parts of it are taking the most processing time. This is great as it informs us whether it's our application, database, or even a third-party API call that's slow. We might not see any potential problems initially, but the issues should be more obvious when our application is under load.

How it works...

New Relic will be crucial when understanding the results of our load tests. Here, we learned the specific steps for the installation of New Relic in a Rails application, but it is available for almost any web stack. We should be using it for any production-level application that we deploy to Heroku.

The New Relic gem records detailed information about each request and sends it to New Relic's API for storage. By default, this data is only sent when our `RAILS_ENV` environment variable is set to production. We can fully configure New Relic by adding a `config/new_relic.yml` file to our application. For more information on how to do this, visit `https://docs.newrelic.com/docs/ruby/ruby-agent-installation`.

See also

► For more general information on getting started with New Relic, visit `https://docs.newrelic.com/docs/help`

Learning to load test with Siege

Siege is an open source application that simulates a massive burst in traffic by sending a configurable number of concurrent connections to our application. It's a perfect way to get introduced to executing a basic load test. There are many load-testing services available, but it's useful to be able to execute one on our own with just a laptop. It's also a nice bonus as it's completely free.

In this recipe, we will learn how to install Siege and then run a load test against our application. Siege has an abundance of different configuration options; we'll learn how to use them. In this recipe, we will be pushing our app to a limit and can have some fun with load testing. We shouldn't run this against a production application; it's fairly easy to overload an application with Siege. We wouldn't want to interrupt any real users because of a test.

Getting ready

First, we'll need to download Siege and get it installed on our machine using the following steps:

1. Let's start by downloading Siege from the project's main website. Fire up a terminal and enter the following command to grab the file:

   ```
   $ curl -O http://download.joedog.org/siege/siege-3.0.7.tar.gz
   ```

    Version 3.0.7 was the latest one at the time of writing this book. There might be a newer version available; each release is documented at `http://www.joedog.org/siege-home/`.

2. Now that it's downloaded, we'll need to unpack the `tar` file:

   ```
   $ tar xzvf siege-3.0.7.tar.gz
   $ cd siege-3.0.7
   ```

3. We're now ready to install Siege. Let's run the following commands to complete the installation:

   ```
   $ ./configure
   $ make
   $ make install
   ```

    Are the commands not working? Make sure you're in the `siege-3.0.7` directory before running them.

4. We should now have Siege installed. We can verify our installation by trying to run Siege:

   ```
   $ siege
   ```

   If this is successful, we will see help information printed on our screen. We're now ready to start running load tests with Siege.

 Having trouble with installation? Take a look at the `INSTALL` file in the root directory of the Siege download. It has more detailed instructions on the installation and some basic information on troubleshooting.

How to do it...

We can now start load testing our application from the command line using Siege by performing the following steps:

1. For our first test, let's pass the URL of our application to Siege, and it will start a test using its default settings. Siege will begin flooding our app with requests immediately. We can stop the requests at any time by pressing *Ctrl + C*:

    > To not affect performance for real users, it's best to run load tests in a staging environment.

    ```
    $ siege http://your-app-name.herokuapp.com

    ** SIEGE 3.0.7
    ** Preparing 15 concurrent users for battle.
    The server is now under siege...
    HTTP/1.1 200     0.10 secs:    16802 bytes ==> GET   /
    HTTP/1.1 200     0.09 secs:    16817 bytes ==> GET   /
    HTTP/1.1 200     0.10 secs:    16823 bytes ==> GET   /
    HTTP/1.1 200     0.16 secs:    16835 bytes ==> GET   /
    HTTP/1.1 200     0.11 secs:    16842 bytes ==> GET   /
    HTTP/1.1 200     0.11 secs:    16838 bytes ==> GET   /
    HTTP/1.1 200     0.11 secs:    16837 bytes ==> GET   /
    HTTP/1.1 200     0.11 secs:    16818 bytes ==> GET   /
    HTTP/1.1 200     0.11 secs:    16831 bytes ==> GET   /
    HTTP/1.1 200     0.10 secs:    16818 bytes ==> GET   /
    HTTP/1.1 200     0.10 secs:    16827 bytes ==> GET   /
    HTTP/1.1 200     0.10 secs:    16808 bytes ==> GET   /
    HTTP/1.1 200     0.11 secs:    16815 bytes ==> GET   /
    ^C
    Lifting the server siege...       done.

    Transactions:                  34 hits
    Availability:              100.00 %
    Elapsed time:                1.90 secs
    Data transferred:            0.28 MB
    Response time:               0.11 secs
    ```

```
Transaction rate:              17.89 trans/sec
Throughput:                    0.15 MB/sec
Concurrency:                   2.05
Successful transactions:         44
Failed transactions:              0
Longest transaction:           0.16
Shortest transaction:          0.05
```

After stopping Siege, we'll see a summary of our test. The key metrics for us to look at will be `Transaction Rate` and `Response Time`. By comparing these two metrics across tests, we will be able to easily see how the increased traffic is affecting our application's performance.

2. Siege has a resource file that stores its configuration settings. We can find out where the resource file is stored with the `-C` flag:

```
$ siege -C
CURRENT  SIEGE  CONFIGURATION
Mozilla/5.0 (apple-x86_64-darwin14.0.0) Siege/3.0.7
Edit the resource file to change the settings.
-----------------------------------------------
version:                       3.0.7
verbose:                       true
quiet:                         false
debug:                         false
protocol:                      HTTP/1.1
get method:                    HEAD
connection:                    close
concurrent users:              15
time to run:                   n/a
repetitions:                   n/a
socket timeout:                30
accept-encoding:               gzip
delay:                         1 sec
internet simulation:           false
benchmark mode:                false
failures until abort:          1024
named URL:                     none
```

URLs file:	/usr/local/etc/urls.txt
logging:	true
log file:	/usr/local/var/siege.log
resource file:	/usr/local/etc/siegerc
timestamped output:	false
comma separated output:	false
allow redirects:	true
allow zero byte data:	true
allow chunked encoding:	true
upload unique files:	true

In this example, our Siege resource file is located at /usr/local/etc/siegerc. Going forward, we will be editing this file to make configuration changes to Siege.

3. Let's set the runtime of our next test to 1 minute. We can do this by opening /usr/local/etc/siegerc and adding the following code:

    ```
    time = 1m
    ```

4. Now, let's run the same command as we did earlier. This time it will run for 1 minute:

    ```
    $ siege http://your-app-name.herokuapp.com
    ```

 Instead of modifying the resource file, we can also set the runtime directly in the command, using the t flag:

```
$ siege http://your-app-name.herokuapp.com -t 1m
```

5. Our current test is simulating 15 concurrent users. Let's put more stress on our application by increasing the number of users to 25. We can use either the -c flag in the Siege command or add concurrent=25 to the resource file. Let's try it here using the flag:

    ```
    $ siege http://your-app-name.herokuapp.com -c 25
    ```

 This can be fairly taxing for some applications. It's possible that we'll see failures at this point.

6. We can experiment by adjusting both the concurrent users and the time of the load test. With high enough values, we will be able to overwhelm our Heroku application. If our application fails, we'll start seeing H11 (backlog too deep) or H12 (request time out) errors.

    The next command should easily overwhelm an application that runs on only one dyno:

    ```
    $ siege http://your-app-name.herokuapp.com -c 600 -t 1m
    ```

    We should quickly start seeing connection errors from Siege that look like the following code:

    ```
    [error] socket: read error Connection reset by peer sock.c:479:
    Connection reset by peer
    ```

    This is great because it gives us an idea of the upper limit our application can handle. We now have a baseline that we can work on beating by optimizing our application.

How it works...

Siege floods our application with concurrent HTTP requests. This simulates what it is like to have a surge of traffic visit our application. It isn't necessarily the most realistic load test but does provide us with a quick way to load test from our own machine. One of the key metrics that Siege reports is concurrency. Concurrency is calculated by taking the total number of requests sent and dividing it by the number of seconds that the test ran. This gives us the average number of requests our application was serving in parallel.

We can use Siege to quickly compare the performance of different dyno formations. By experimenting with the number and size of our dynos, we can get an idea of the costs associated with different levels of performance.

See also

We've just begun with Siege; move on to the next recipe to learn about more advanced configurations. You can also refer to the following:

▸   The Siege home page at `http://www.joedog.org/siege-home/`
▸   Siege FAQ at `http://www.joedog.org/siege-faq/`

Configuring complex load tests with Siege

In the previous recipe, we learned how to install Siege, configure it, and run our first tests. Siege has many more configuration options that we can use to create more realistic load tests. In this recipe, we will learn how to have Siege attack multiple URLs in our application, as well as send POST requests. We'll see how to randomize the requests that get sent to make it mimic real-life scenarios more closely.

How to do it...

Let's fire up a terminal to get started by performing the following steps:

1. We can configure Siege to attack more than a single URL by editing Siege's URL file. To find out where this file is stored, we'll need to check our configuration:

```
$ siege -C
CURRENT   SIEGE   CONFIGURATION
Mozilla/5.0 (apple-x86_64-darwin14.0.0) Siege/3.0.7
Edit the resource file to change the settings.
-------------------------------------------------

version:                  3.0.7
verbose:                  true
quiet:                    false
debug:                    false
protocol:                 HTTP/1.1
get method:               HEAD
connection:               close
concurrent users:         15
time to run:              n/a
repetitions:              n/a
socket timeout:           30
accept-encoding:          gzip
delay:                    1 sec
internet simulation:      false
benchmark mode:           false
failures until abort:     1024
named URL:                none
```

```
URLs file:                     /usr/local/etc/urls.txt
logging:                       true
log file:                      /usr/local/var/siege.log
resource file:                 /usr/local/etc/siegerc
timestamped output:            false
comma separated output:        false
allow redirects:               true
allow zero byte data:          true
allow chunked encoding:        true
upload unique files:           true
```

2. Now that we know where our URL's file is, we can add a couple of different URLs to it to test different parts of our application.

    Siege will send a GET request to each of these URLs. Each URL needs to be separated by a new line:

    ```
    http://your-app-name.herokuapp.com/
    ```

    ```
    http://your-app-name.herokuapp.com/posts
    ```

    ```
    http://your-app-name.herokuapp.com/pages/about
    ```

    Once the URLs are added, we can run Siege, and we'll see that it sends requests to the different pages we listed.

     Remember that the -c flag defines the concurrent users, and the -t flag is the length of the test.

    Run the following command:

    ```
    $ siege -c 100 -t 30s
    HTTP/1.1 200   0.17 secs:    15633 bytes ==> GET  /posts
    HTTP/1.1 200   0.14 secs:    15633 bytes ==> GET  /posts
    HTTP/1.1 200   0.13 secs:     2638 bytes ==> GET  /
    HTTP/1.1 200   0.12 secs:     2780 bytes ==> GET  /pages/about
    HTTP/1.1 200   0.07 secs:     2779 bytes ==> GET  /pages/about
    HTTP/1.1 200   0.08 secs:     2779 bytes ==> GET  /pages/about
    HTTP/1.1 200   0.15 secs:    15633 bytes ==> GET  /posts
    HTTP/1.1 200   0.09 secs:     2636 bytes ==> GET  /
    HTTP/1.1 200   0.09 secs:     2779 bytes ==> GET  /pages/about
    ```

```
HTTP/1.1 200    0.11 secs:    2780 bytes ==> GET  /pages/about
HTTP/1.1 200    0.16 secs:   15633 bytes ==> GET  /posts
HTTP/1.1 200    0.08 secs:    2779 bytes ==> GET  /pages/about
```

From the output of the test, we can see that Siege sent requests to each of the URLs in our URL's file. With this, we can create load tests that are little closer to the real-world usage of our application.

3. We can have Siege randomize the order in which it hits each URL using the Internet flag.

   Let's try the same test again, but with the `-i` flag:

   ```
   $ siege -i -c 100 -t 30s
   ```

4. Now that we are flooding our application with random GET requests, let's add a POST request that will stress it even further.

   We'll need a URL in our application that responds to a POST request. A good example will be somewhere in the application where the user submits some data. We can set up Siege to send this data.

   Let's open up our URL's file and add another line to it in the following format:

   ```
   http://your-app-name.herokuapp.com/posts/new POST firstname=Aaron
   content=Test
   ```

   The end of the line contains any query parameters that our application needs to complete the request. In this example, the application needs two variables to complete the request: `firstname` and `content`.

> The parameters for the POST request will depend on the specific application. It might take a few attempts to get it right. Siege will display the response code, and the `-v` flag can be used to see a more verbose output to debug.

5. Let's run this test again with our new POST request added to the file:

   ```
   $ siege -i -c 100 -t 30s
   HTTP/1.1 200    0.18 secs:   16430 bytes ==> GET  /posts
   HTTP/1.1 201 0.08 secs:   1334 bytes ==> POST http://your-app-name.
   herokuapp.com/posts/new POST firstname=Aaron content=Test
   HTTP/1.1 200    0.22 secs:   16430 bytes ==> GET  /posts
   HTTP/1.1 200    0.08 secs:    2625 bytes ==> GET  /
   ```

   In our test output, we will now see that Siege is making POST as well as GET requests.

While a load test is running, it can be useful to watch our application's logs. To do so, open up another terminal window and run `$ heroku logs --tail --app application_name`.

How it works...

We're now able to configure Siege to complete more complex tests for us. Siege is highly configurable through both its configuration file and URL file. We've learned enough here; we will now be able to cover most use cases of Siege to load test.

We can get the most out of this by running our tests for long time periods and observing how our monitoring services react to the stress of the load test. We should be viewing CPU and memory usage in Librato and examining slow transactions in New Relic to take full advantage of our load-testing efforts.

Load testing from the cloud with Blitz.io

To load test on a larger scale, we'll need to use a cloud-based service that is capable of sending a massive volume of concurrent requests to our application. Blitz.io is one of the leading cloud load-testing tools. It is highly configurable and allows us to send requests from multiple locations throughout the world. With Blitz, we can more closely imitate real-user traffic by ramping up the number of visitors over a period of time. This allows us to see the upper limit of our current infrastructure. Having this knowledge allows us to prepare for any events where we will be expecting a large volume of visitors.

Getting ready

Before we start load testing with Blitz, we'll need to install the add-on using the following steps:

1. Let's open up a terminal and navigate to the Heroku application that we want to load test. Then, we can add Blitz by running the following command:

   ```
   $ heroku addons:add blitz
   ```

2. After installing the add-on, we can use the open command to launch the Blitz dashboard. We'll see that our Heroku application has already been set up to load test:

   ```
   $ heroku addons:open blitz
   ```

How to do it...

Blitz.io is very developer-focused. In its user interface, we'll see that it has two different versions: a simple interface and a more advanced one that closely mimics cURL commands. We'll be using the simple interface here. It has all of the same capabilities of the cURL interface and is easier to learn.

There are three types of tests we can perform. A sprint sends a single request to our application and reports back the response time. A rush is a load test that simulates a large volume of concurrent users who visit our application. A performance test is a single request that loads our application in a browser and shows a breakdown of all the HTTP requests made to load the page. This is done as follows:

1. To start, let's open the Blitz dashboard it if it isn't already open:

    ```
    $ heroku addons:open blitz
    ```

2. Now that we're at the dashboard, let's click on the silver play button to start creating our first test.

3. For our first test, let's run a simple sprint to make sure everything is working. We can do this by clicking in the URL text area and selecting our authorized domain. It should be prepopulated for us. Then, let's select **SPRINT** and click on the large arrow button to start the test.

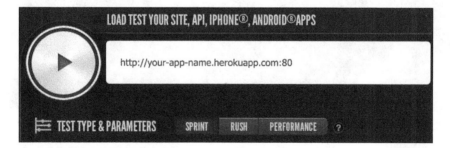

 Notice **:80** at the end of the URL. This is the port number for the application. Standard HTTP requests use port 80. HTTPS requests use port 443.

4. Once we have successfully completed a sprint, we can try out our first load test by running a rush. With a rush, we are able to specify the starting and ending numbers of concurrent users who visit our app. This is meant to simulate a sudden increase in traffic. If our application is running on a single dyno, the default setting of 250 is very likely to overwhelm our application. Fifty users is a more reasonable setting for our first test.

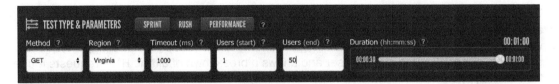

As the load test runs, we'll see a graph of how our application responds to the increased load. These results will be saved to our account so that we can access them again at any time. It might be helpful to fill in the **MY NOTES** section with details of the number and size of dynos that were present while testing. It makes it easier to go back later on and remember exactly what was tested.

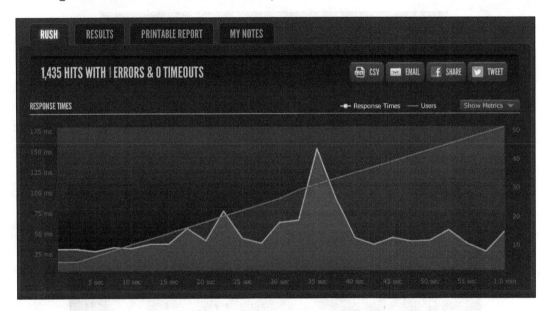

5. We should keep running rushes until we find our application's upper limit. This will give us a baseline for performance; we can compare this baseline as we work on optimizing our application.

How it works...

Blitz is similar to Siege in that it floods our application with web requests. The advantage of using Blitz over Siege is in the capacity, location, and ease of use. Blitz can run larger load tests than Siege and can test from multiple locations throughout the world. This makes it easy to see how our application's response time differs from different regions.

In this recipe, we just did a basic sprint and rushed to get started. Blitz can do more advanced tests that can easily be set up from the same screen. We can run multistep tests that send a variety of HTTP requests to our application in an effort to model real user activity more closely.

See also

▶   The Blitz documentation is very useful when getting started or trying to implement more complex scenarios. Take a look at `https://www.blitz.io/docs/overview`.

Testing real-user scenarios with Load Impact

So far, we have explored how to push our application to the brink of failure by attacking it with massive floods of concurrent requests. The load tests created with Siege and Blitz are helpful in finding performance bottlenecks in our application, but they do not exactly replicate real-world situations. Normal site usage will usually follow a few different patterns. For example, let's imagine a typical e-commerce web application. There are probably three main usages of the application. Ninety percent of the application's users are most likely browsing the home page or the product catalog. Another 5 percent of the users are going through the checkout process, and the final 5 percent might be viewing order or account information. By recreating these scenarios, we can get an accurate view of how our application will behave for real users.

In this recipe, we will be introduced to Load Impact, a load-testing tool that will allow us to mimic real-world traffic by creating and testing different user scenarios.

Getting ready

To begin, we'll need to set up a Load Impact account using the following steps:

1.   Let's head over to `http://www.loadimpact.com` and sign up.

2.   We'll use Google Chrome to set up our Load Impact scenarios. Load Impact has a great Chrome extension that makes it easy to record user scenarios in our browser. We can install it through the Chrome store at `https://chrome.google.com/webstore/detail/load-impact-user-scenario/comniomddgkfgfaebhidfgcjgoecbbda`.

3. We'll need to activate the Chrome extension by entering our Load Impact API token. We can get the key by going to our account page (`https://loadimpact.com/account`) and clicking on **Generate a new token**.

4. Now that the Chrome extension is activated, we're ready to start generating scenarios.

How to do it...

We'll start by using the Load Impact Chrome extension to create our first load test scenario by performing the following steps:

1. Let's open up Chrome and navigate to the web application we want to load test. Once we're on the page, we can start generating a scenario by opening the Load Impact extension and clicking on **Start Recording**.

2. Now, we can start using our application, and the Chrome extension will record everything we do in the browser. Load Impact will repeat these steps later during our load test. Once we're done with the recording, we'll need to open the extension again and click on **Stop**.

3. Once the recording is finished, we'll be brought to a page that shows our actions translated into code. Let's give a descriptive name to our scenario and save it:

 We can repeat these steps to create multiple scenarios for use in our load tests. We're not limited to using one scenario.

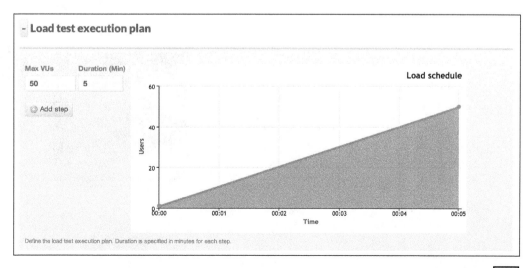

> Scenarios are written in Lua; to learn more about how to write scenarios,
> take a look at Load Impact's documentation on Lua (`http://support.`
> `loadimpact.com/knowledgebase/articles/174637-lua-`
> `quick-start-guide`).

4. Now that we have at least one scenario set up, we can start testing our application. Let's navigate to the Load Impact dashboard (`https://loadimpact.com/test/list`); go to **Test configurations** and click on **Create test configuration**.

5. We will need to fill in our application's URL and then click on **Load test execution plan**. Here, we will select the length of our test and the maximum number of **virtual users** (**VUs**) that Load Impact will use to run through our scenarios.

6. Next, we'll need to select the scenarios we want our test to use. We will be able to pick from any of the scenarios we generated earlier with the Chrome extension. We can also specify the percentage of users for each scenario as well as the geographical origin of the traffic.

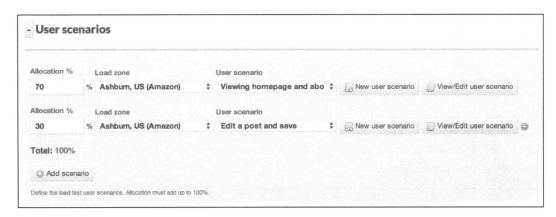

7. Finally, we can start our test by scrolling to the bottom of the page and clicking on **Create test configuration and start test**. Our test will start running, and we'll immediately see results populating the screen.

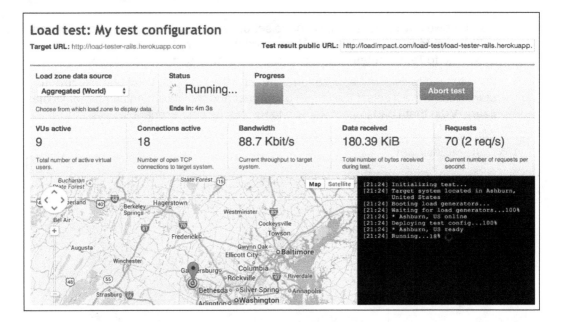

While running load tests, remember to keep an eye on your monitoring tools. They will provide insight into how the application is responding and help point out areas for improvement.

How it works...

Load Impact is as close as we can get to simulating real users on our Heroku application. Most load-testing tools send simple HTTP GET requests to our application. This is similar to using cURL on the command line to send a request. Load Impact tests our application by simulating a user's browser session and then automating the user's interactions with our application.

We used the Chrome extension to generate basic scenarios to test. If we view the scenarios we created, we'll see that they are written in Lua. We can use these scenarios as a starting point to learn to write more advanced tests. Load Impact is not used exclusively to load test; it can also be used to verify the functionality of our web application and be included in our testing and deployment process.

See also

- ▶ Check out Load Impact's support site at `http://support.loadimpact.com/` for details on how to create more advanced testing scenarios
- ▶ For help with troubleshooting common issues, take a look at Load Impact's documentation at `http://support.loadimpact.com/knowledgebase/articles/173855-problems-when-running-load-tests`

7

Optimizing Ruby Server Performance on Heroku

In this chapter, we will cover:

- ▶ Setting up and running Unicorn on Heroku
- ▶ Monitoring and tuning Unicorn's memory usage
- ▶ Tuning Unicorn's backlog for Heroku
- ▶ Timing out long requests with Unicorn
- ▶ Setting up and running Puma on Heroku
- ▶ Running Puma with Rubinius for parallelism

Introduction

We have several great options to choose from when picking a web server to run our Ruby applications. Newer developers will typically start out using WEBrick, which is the default web server for Rails and Rack applications. WEBrick is great when developing or testing an application, but it falls short quickly when we need to serve real production traffic. The main problem with using WEBrick is its lack of concurrency. It's only able to process a single request at a time. This is very limiting and forces us to spin up multiple dynos to handle even a modest amount of traffic.

In this chapter, we will be introduced to Unicorn and Puma, two web servers that are great options to run production-level Ruby applications on Heroku. Each provides us with the concurrency we need to run a high-traffic web application. Depending on our application's memory footprint, both Unicorn and Puma will provide us with a performance boost over WEBrick; this boost will range from 2 to 4X. This results in us being able to serve more requests per dyno, reducing the total number of dynos that we need to run our applications.

Setting up and running Unicorn on Heroku

For Ruby applications on Heroku, Unicorn should be our default choice when picking a web server. When Unicorn starts up, it forks our application's process. Each fork is known as a **worker process**. Each one of these processes are able to respond to web requests. The more processes we run, the more concurrency will be available on a single dyno.

As each worker is its own process, it has its own memory space, so we do not need to worry about our application's code being thread safe. This makes Unicorn a good choice for developers who are unsure whether their application can handle threading.

How to do it...

To begin, we will need to set up our existing Rails application to run Unicorn.

 If you'd like to skip this setup, you can use an example application available on GitHub at `https://github.com/mscoutermarsh/unicorn-rails-heroku`. This application is already set up to use Unicorn on Heroku.

Perform the following steps:

1. First, we'll need to add Unicorn to our gemfile. Let's open up our project's gemfile and add the following line:

   ```
   gem 'unicorn'
   ```

2. Next, we'll need to run `bundle install`:

   ```
   $ bundle install
   ```

3. We'll need to set up a configuration file specific to Unicorn. Let's create a new file in `config/unicorn.rb` and paste it in the following code:

   ```
   # config/unicorn.rb

   worker_processes Integer(ENV['WEB_CONCURRENCY'] || 3)
   timeout Integer(ENV['WEB_TIMEOUT'] || 15)
   preload_app true


   before_fork do |server, worker|

     Signal.trap 'TERM' do
   ```

```
    puts 'Unicorn master intercepting TERM and sending myself QUIT
instead'
    Process.kill 'QUIT', Process.pid
  end


  defined?(ActiveRecord::Base) and
    ActiveRecord::Base.connection.disconnect!
end


after_fork do |server, worker|

  Signal.trap 'TERM' do
    puts 'Unicorn worker intercepting TERM and doing nothing. Wait
for master to send QUIT'
  end


  defined?(ActiveRecord::Base) and
    ActiveRecord::Base.establish_connection
end
```

 This config file is also available on GitHub at `https://github.com/mscoutermarsh/unicorn-rails-heroku/blob/master/config/unicorn.rb`.

4. We will need to tell Heroku how to start our application that runs Unicorn. We will do this using a Procfile. In the root directory of our project, create a file named `Procfile` with the help of the following line:

   ```
   web: bundle exec unicorn -p $PORT -c ./config/unicorn.rb
   ```

5. Next, let's commit our changes to Git:

   ```
   $ git add .
   $ git commit -m 'setting up unicorn'
   ```

6. The last step is pushing this application to Heroku. If this is an existing production application, we should first try it out on a staging or testing environment. Changing web servers is a major step and issues may pop up:

   ```
   $ git push heroku master
   ```

7. Now that it is deployed, let's take a look at our running processes. We should see that our web dynos are running Unicorn:

```
$ heroku ps
Process  State      Command
-------  ---------  ------------------------------------
web.1    up for 6s  bundle exec unicorn -p $PORT -c ./..
```

How it works

The configuration file we defined in this recipe is what Unicorn's master process uses to handle forking and manage our Unicorn workers. There are two blocks of code that we should pay particular attention to: `before_fork` and `after_fork`. These blocks run before and after the forking process. In our configuration, we use these blocks to manage our application's database connections. This ensures that we are not leaving extra connections open or starting a new process without establishing a new connection. In this example, we are only dropping and creating connections for ActiveRecord. If our application establishes connections to other services, we might need to add logic here to handle these connections as well.

 Each Unicorn process will use its own database connection, which is important for us to remember if our database has small number of available connections.

See also

▸   To learn more about Unicorn, visit the project's home page at `http://unicorn.bogomips.org/`

Monitoring and tuning Unicorn's memory usage

Our main constraint when running multiple Unicorn workers is the memory available on the dyno. A typical application will use somewhere between 50 and 200 MB of memory per process. We want to configure our application to use between 50 to 70 percent of the available memory on a dyno. This gives our processes room to grow while still using most of the resources we are paying for.

In this recipe, we will be learning how to determine how much memory our application uses per Unicorn process. We will then be tweaking our configuration to maximize concurrency within a single dyno.

We want to avoid running too close to 100 percent memory usage. If we run out of memory, our dyno will start using swap. This should be avoided at all costs. Using any swap will greatly decrease the performance of the dyno and response times will skyrocket.

How to do it...

To get started, let's open up a terminal and navigate to the directory with our Unicorn application using the following steps:

1. First, we need to determine how much memory each Unicorn process is using. We can do this by enabling log-runtime-metrics:

```
$ heroku labs:enable log-runtime-metrics
$ heroku restart
```

2. We can now take a look at our logs, and we'll see our memory usage printed for each dyno:

```
$ heroku logs --tail
sample#memory_rss=230.39MB
```

 In the logs, we'll see different measurements for memory. We might want to look at memory_rss, which is the amount of RAM being used. Other values, such as memory_total, also include any swap. Memory_swap should always be zero; if it's not, we need to reduce the number of workers we're using.

3. Next, we need to know how many Unicorn processes we currently have running. We can do this by looking at the WEB_CONCURRENCY configuration variable:

```
$ heroku config:get WEB_CONCURRENCY
=> 3
```

 If WEB_CONCURRENCY is not set, Unicorn will run three processes by default. The default is set in our unicorn.rb initializer.

4. Now that we know our dyno's memory usage and how many processes we're running, we can do a little math to determine how much RAM is used by a single process. In this example, we're running three unicorn workers, and the application is using 230 MB of RAM. So, each process uses around 77 MB of RAM.

Memory usage will vary between a cold and warm application. We should check memory usage after a dyno has been running and processing requests for a while.

5. We're now ready to adjust our application's concurrency. For a 1X dyno, we want to target using no more than 375 MB of the total memory. For a 2X dyno, we can go up to 725 MB.

   As this example application is using 77 MB per process and we're using 1X dynos, 4 Unicorn processes should get us to around 308 MB of RAM; this is as close as we can get to 375 MB for this application.

6. Let's adjust the application's concurrency now by changing the configuration variable:

   ```
   $ heroku config:set WEB_CONCURRENCY=4
   ```

7. Now that we've adjusted the concurrency, we should continue to monitor our dyno's memory usage. In this example, we've left it with plenty of room to grow, but it's a good practice to keep an eye on it. Tools such as New Relic and Librato make it easy to monitor memory usage over longer periods of time.

How it works...

In our `config/unicorn.rb` file, we set the unicorn concurrency to either the value of the `WEB_CONCURRENCY` environment variable or to a default value of 3. By adding this to our Unicorn configuration, it makes it easy to adjust the concurrency without having to change any code. After any configuration change, Heroku will restart all of our dynos, and they will boot up using the new settings. These settings are also tied to release management; this allows us to roll back and have a record of any and all configuration changes to our application.

It will take a couple attempts to get the correct Unicorn concurrency set for an application. After changing it, we should watch closely to see how it reacts in production use. Some applications may have memory leaks that slowly expand the processes' size over time. When running near the maximum memory threshold for a dyno, memory leaks become more dangerous and put us as risk for swap. Heroku dynos are replaced by new dynos every 24 hours, giving us some protection from slow memory leaks. It can be useful to set up memory monitoring with Librato, to monitor memory usage over a 24-hour period to ensure that we do not get close to that limit.

See also

▶ For more information on monitoring memory usage, take a look at the *Monitoring Dyno Performance with Librato* recipe in *Chapter 6, Load Testing a Heroku Application*

Tuning Unicorn's backlog for Heroku

A single dyno that runs Unicorn can serve as many concurrent requests as it has Unicorn workers available. A dyno that runs four Unicorn workers can serve a maximum of four requests at a time. If our dyno receives more than four concurrent requests, it will add the extra requests to a queue and process them once a worker is available.

This can be problematic on Heroku due to how Heroku routes requests to dynos. Heroku's router sends requests randomly to any dyno that does not have a full backlog. Ideally, we'd like Heroku to route requests to the dyno that is most capable of serving the request quickly. The default setting for Unicorn's backlog is 1024 requests. This means that a Unicorn dyno can have a queue of 1,024 requests before Heroku will stop sending requests to it.

In this recipe, we will learn how to reduce our Unicorn backlog to keep requests from piling up on a single dyno and have Heroku reroute our requests to a dyno with available capacity.

How to do it...

To start, let's open up a terminal and navigate to our Rails project running Heroku. We will be editing our `config/unicorn.rb` file to change Unicorn's backlog using the following steps:

1. In our `unicorn.rb` file, let's find the line that defines our request timeout:

   ```
   timeout Integer(ENV['WEB_TIMEOUT'] || 15)
   ```

   Then, after this, let's add the following code. This is what will set our Unicorn backlog:

   ```
   listen ENV['PORT'], backlog: Integer(ENV['UNICORN_BACKLOG'] || 50)
   ```

   > To see an example on GitHub, take a look at `https://github.com/mscoutermarsh/unicorn-rails-heroku/blob/backlog_tuning/config/unicorn.rb#L5`.

2. Next, we can update our `Procfile` as we are now specifying the port in our Unicorn `config` file. Let's replace what we have for our web process with the following code:

   ```
   web: bundle exec unicorn -c ./config/unicorn.rb
   ```

3. That's it for code changes. Now, let's commit the changes and push them up to Heroku:

   ```
   $ git add Procfile
   $ git add config/unicorn.rb
   $ git commit -m 'Adding backlog configuration to Unicorn'
   $ git push heroku master
   ```

Be careful! Any change to the web server can be risky. Make sure that you test it in a staging environment before pushing it to production.

4. In the preceding code, we set our default backlog to 50. We also conveniently added a method to control the backlog via an environment variable so that we can tweak our configuration without making any more code changes. Now, we can adjust our backlog setting with the following command:

```
$ heroku config:set UNICORN_BACKLOG=16
```

How it works...

When Unicorn's backlog reaches its maximum length, it refuses requests from the Heroku router until it is able to accept them again. This will make Heroku reroute the request to another one of our dynos.

Under very high traffic, it is possible for all of our dynos to be overwhelmed with requests. If all of our dynos have a full backlog, Heroku will continue trying to route the request. However, it will eventually stop trying and return an H11 "Backlog too deep" error.

If we have log monitoring enabled through a service such as LogEntries, we'd be alerted immediately that a user received this error, and we could scale up our dynos to respond to the increase in traffic. This situation will most likely be very rare, and if we have proper monitoring in place, an increase in traffic should not catch us by surprise.

Setting our Unicorn backlog to a low number helps us ensure that our users are receiving a consistent response time from our application. Their requests will never be stuck waiting behind a large queue of other users, and Heroku will know which dynos cannot handle any more requests.

Finding the correct backlog setting can be tricky. It's best to be very aggressive and start with a low number (such as 16). The New Relic add-on allows us to see the amount of time our requests are spend in queue. This gives us visibility into how quickly Heroku is able to route requests to our dynos. By running load tests against multiple dynos, we can monitor the queue time to learn what backlog setting works best for our application.

See also

▶ To learn more about tuning Unicorn, refer to Unicorn's documentation at http://unicorn.bogomips.org/TUNING.html.

▶ In this recipe, we used the listen method to configure our backlog setting. To read more about listen, take a look at http://unicorn.bogomips.org/Unicorn/Configurator.html#method-i-listen.

Timing out long requests with Unicorn

A web application's throughput is dependent on the number of concurrent requests it can serve as well as how quickly it can serve each of these requests. An application will be able to handle most web requests very quickly and move on to serving the next request. However, what happens if a single request takes 10, 20, or even 30 seconds to complete? The Unicorn worker processing that request will be unable to take on another one until its current long-running request is complete. Under normal traffic, this would probably be fine. Another Unicorn worker will pick up the incoming requests, but it becomes a problem when an application needs to be processing a high number of requests very quickly.

In this recipe, we will learn how to timeout long-running requests to keep them from tying up resources and hurting our application's throughput.

How to do it...

To get started, let's open up a terminal and navigate to our Rails application that runs Unicorn by performing the following steps:

1. For this, we will be taking advantage of the environment variables we previously added to our `config/unicorn.rb` file. Let's open the file and take a look at it. Take a look at the following line:

   ```
   timeout Integer(ENV['WEB_TIMEOUT'] || 15)
   ```

   This line sets the maximum running time for a request. Here, we are setting it to the value of the WEB_TIMEOUT environment variable, or if this is not set, it defaults to 15 seconds.

2. To change our timeout, all we need to do is update the environment variable. Heroku's own timeout is set to 30 seconds, so let's make Unicorn stop requests a little sooner than this:

   ```
   $ heroku config:set WEB_TIMEOUT=25
   ```

How it works...

Heroku will show the user an error message for any request that takes longer than 30 seconds to respond. Even though the user has already received a response, the request could still be processing on the dyno. This takes up resources and is useless since the user will never see the result. A timeout period of 30 seconds is generously long to begin with. Our applications should never have requests processing for that long; it ties up resources, and having more than one of these requests running concurrently can bring our application to a halt.

Unicorn's timeout will stop the actual processing of the request. This allows us to stop the process and return an error message simultaneously.

Stopping requests in this method should be thought of as a safety switch for our application. It should be very rare that we ever have long-running requests, but just in case it does happen, we can have Unicorn stopping them from causing too much damage.

See also

▶ For more information on how Heroku handles timeouts, take a look at the documentation on the H12 error at `https://devcenter.heroku.com/articles/error-codes#h12-request-timeout`

Setting up and running Puma on Heroku

Puma is a lightweight Ruby web server that was built for concurrency. It is a great alternative to Unicorn and works well on Heroku. Like Unicorn, Puma allows us to get more performance out of our dynos by responding to multiple requests simultaneously. It does this while maintaining a smaller memory footprint than Unicorn and has shown very impressive benchmarks when load tested.

The primary difference between Puma and Unicorn is that Puma will run multiple threads within a single process. This is an important distinction, because while processes have their own unique memory space, threads do not. This means our application's code must be thread safe.

The danger of code that is not thread safe is that separate web requests could be reading and writing from the same memory. This can cause errors or, worse, display data that was intended for another user.

How to do it...

To start, we'll need an existing Rails application running on Heroku. We'll modify it here to run Puma.

 If you need an application to try this out on, try taking our example Unicorn application from `https://github.com/mscoutermarsh/unicorn-rails-heroku` and converting it to run on Puma.

1. First, we'll need to add the Puma gem to our application's Gemfile. If we currently have any other web server in our Gemfile (such as Unicorn), we'll have to delete it since we're replacing it with Puma:

    ```
    gem 'puma'
    ```

2. Next, we'll run `bundle install` to download Puma and update `Gemfile.lock`:

```
$ bundle install
```

3. Now, we'll need to update our `Procfile` so that Heroku knows how to use Puma when starting our application. Replace the existing web command with the following code:

```
web: bundle exec puma -C config/puma.rb
```

 If you were previously using Unicorn in this application, remember to remove your Unicorn configuration file, `config/unicorn.rb`.

4. We'll need to create a new configuration file for Puma. Let's do this by creating a new file in `config/puma.rb`. Paste it in the following code:

```
workers Integer(ENV['PUMA_WORKERS'] || 3)
threads Integer(ENV['MIN_THREADS']  || 1), Integer(ENV['MAX_
THREADS'] || 16)

preload_app!

rackup        DefaultRackup

port = Integer(ENV['PORT'] || 3000)
backlog = Integer(ENV['PUMA_BACKLOG'] || 20)

bind "tcp://0.0.0.0:#{port}?backlog=#{backlog}"

environment ENV['RACK_ENV'] || 'development'

on_worker_boot do
  # worker specific setup
  ActiveSupport.on_load(:active_record) do
    config = ActiveRecord::Base.configurations[Rails.env] ||
Rails.application.config.database_configuration[Rails.env]
    config['pool'] = ENV['MAX_THREADS'] || 16
    ActiveRecord::Base.establish_connection(config)
  end
end
```

This file is also available on GitHub at `https://github.com/mscoutermarsh/puma_heroku_example/blob/master/config/puma.rb`.

5. Now that our configuration is all set, we can commit the changes and push them up to Heroku. This is a major change, so we should test it out on a staging application first:

```
$ git add config/puma.rb
$ git commit -am "Setting up application to run on Puma"
$ git push heroku master
```

 To see a complete example application with the Puma setup for Heroku, take a look at this project on GitHub at `https://github.com/mscoutermarsh/puma_heroku_example`.

6. In the configuration file, there were references to environment variables that we can use to tweak our Puma config:

   ❑ `PUMA_WORKERS`: This refers to the number of processes that Puma will spawn. A 1X dyno will usually be able to run around 2 to 4 of these, depending on the memory usage of the application.

   ❑ `MIN_THREADS`: This is the minimum number of threads that Puma will run within a process. This allows Puma to give up resources when they are not all being utilized. As our Heroku dynos are not shared by other applications, we can set this to be the same as our maximum thread's value.

   ❑ `MAX_THREADS`: This is the maximum number of threads that Puma will run within a single process. Each additional thread has a small memory footprint, but this can affect the total CPU usage. It's also important to note that the application must be thread safe to run multiple threads.

   ❑ `PUMA_BACKLOG`: This is the maximum number of requests that Puma can have in a queue before it refuses more requests from Heroku's router. This number should be low for applications that are running many dynos, as it helps Heroku distribute requests more evenly.

We should set some initial values and then monitor our application's performance. We can then easily tweak the values as needed by updating the environment variables:

```
$ heroku config:set MIN_THREADS=4 MAX_THREADS=4 PUMA_WORKERS=3 PUMA_
BACKLOG=25
```

Ruby's ability to handle threading is dependent on the specific Ruby implementation we are using. To learn more about how the standard MRI handles threading and what the alternatives are, take a look at the *Running Puma with Rubinius for parallelism* recipe.

How it works...

Ruby web server performance is highly dependent on the application. Both Unicorn and Puma are excellent choices to run on Heroku, and we should explore which works best for our application. The key difference is that Puma has concurrency within each process. A single Unicorn process can only respond to one request at a time. A single Puma process can respond to multiple requests. This gives us higher concurrency within a single dyno. Memory usage is primarily driven by the number of individual processes we are running rather than the number of threads within the process. This gives Puma an advantage, as it's able to provide concurrency within a single process.

For us to take advantage of Puma's threading, we need to ensure that our application is thread safe. Rails 4 has thread safety enabled by default, but we also must check whether our own code and the gems that we load are thread safe. For more information on thread safety in Rails applications, visit this blog post from Remarkable Labs at `http://blog. remarkablelabs.com/2012/12/rails-4-is-thread-safe-by-default-rails-4-countdown-to-2013`.

See also

- ▶ Performance benchmarks can be found on Puma's official website at `http://puma.io`
- ▶ For a third-party benchmark, refer to Ylan Segal's comparison of Unicorn and Puma at `http://ylan.segal-family.com/blog/2013/05/20/unicorn-vs-puma-redux/`

Running Puma with Rubinius for parallelism

The Puma web server was built for parallelism, but unfortunately, the standard MRI implementation of Ruby is not. **Rubinius** is an implementation of Ruby that was built with the purpose of solving MRI's concurrency problem. With Rubinius, we will be able to achieve true parallelism in our application. Puma's threaded processes in combination with Rubinius can give our application a huge performance boost. In this recipe, we will learn how to set up our application to run on Rubinius.

How to do it...

To start, we'll need an existing Heroku application that is running on Puma. Specific directions are available in the previous recipe, *Setting up and running Puma on Heroku*:

1. We'll need to install the latest version of Rubinius on our machine. Although there are several Rubinius installation methods, the easiest one is through RVM:

    ```
    $ rvm install rbx-2.2.6
    ```

     At the time of writing this book, rbx-2.2.6 was the latest version. To ensure that we're running the latest version, we can omit the version number from the command and run $ `rvm install rbx`.

    These Rubinius installation directions are specific to RVM; if we do not have the RVM setup, we can visit `https://rvm.io` for more information.

    For help with installation through RVM, visit `https://rvm.io/interpreters/rbx`.

2. After the installation of Rubinius, we can verify that is installed correctly by checking the version:

    ```
    $ rvm use rbx
    $ ruby -v
    rubinius 2.2.6 (2.1.0 68d916a5 2014-03-10 JI) [x86_64-
    darwin13.1.0]
    ```

3. Now that Rubinius is set up, we will need to edit our Gemfile to tell our application to use it. We'll add the following line at the top of our Gemfile:

    ```
    ruby '2.1.0', engine: 'rbx', engine_version: '2.2.6'
    ```

4. We'll need to run `bundle install`:

    ```
    $ bundle install
    ```

5. We're now ready to deploy our application to Heroku. Let's commit it to Git and push our changes:

    ```
    $ git commit -am 'Setting up Rubinius'
    $ git push heroku master
    Fetching repository, done.
    Counting objects: 7, done.
    Delta compression using up to 4 threads.
    Compressing objects: 100% (4/4), done.
    ```

```
Writing objects: 100% (4/4), 479 bytes | 0 bytes/s, done.
Total 4 (delta 3), reused 0 (delta 0)


-----> Ruby app detected
-----> Compiling Ruby/Rails
-----> Using Ruby version: ruby-2.1.0-rbx-2.2.6
-----> Installing dependencies using 1.6.3
       Ruby version change detected. Clearing bundler cache.
       Old: ruby 2.0.0p481 (2014-05-08 revision 45883)
       New: rubinius 2.2.6 (2.1.0 68d916a5 2014-03-10 JI)
```

During the deploy, we will see that Heroku will detect the change in Ruby versions and will deploy using Rubinius instead.

6. As we now have parallelism within processes, we can reduce our Puma workers to one. This will drastically lower our total memory usage:

    ```
    $ heroku config:set PUMA_WORKERS=1
    ```

7. Now, we can try out our application that runs on Rubinius:

    ```
    $ heroku open
    ```

> For a complete working example of Rubinius on Puma, there is a Rubinius branch on our Puma example project at `https://github.com/mscoutermarsh/puma_heroku_example/tree/rubinius`.

How it works...

Ruby MRI (Matz's Ruby Interpreter) is the de facto implementation of the Ruby language. It is almost certainly what we are currently using in all of our Ruby applications on Heroku. Unfortunately, MRI is unable to execute Ruby code in separate threads in parallel. Only one thread can execute Ruby at a time, and once this thread has completed its operation, another thread will be able to use the CPU. This is why we commonly use web servers such as Unicorn to deploy our applications in multiple processes so that we can achieve parallelism.

> We can run processes in parallel because they use their own independent memory space. Threads share memory space, and Ruby blocks parallelism to avoid errors caused by separate threads that attempt to manipulate the same data in memory.

Even though MRI cannot execute Ruby code in parallel threads, threading isn't completely useless to us. MRI can still complete I/O tasks (such as HTTP and database requests) in parallel. Since most web applications are I/O heavy, we can still see a performance boost from running multiple threads. While one thread is waiting for an I/O task to complete, another thread will be able to make use of the CPU.

 The mechanism that stops parallelism in Ruby threads is known as the, **Global Interpreter Lock** (**GIL**). After Version 1.9, it became known as the **Global VM Lock** (**GVL**). They are essentially the same thing.

Rubinius is a Ruby implementation without a GIL. It was built to be thread safe and allow parallel execution of Ruby code. It is a great companion for Puma and has a large and active community behind it.

See also

- The official Rubinius site at `https://rubini.us`
- Rubinius on GitHub at `https://github.com/rubinius/rubinius`
- *Ruby, Concurrency, and You* by Evan Phoenix at `https://blog.engineyard.com/2011/ruby-concurrency-and-you`
- *Rails 4 and the Future of Web* by Aaron Patterson at `https://www.youtube.com/watch?v=kufXhNkm5WU`

8
Optimizing a Rails Application on Heroku

In this chapter, we will cover:

- ► Setting up a sample blogging app
- ► Using Heroku Deflater to gzip assets
- ► Serving assets from Amazon Web Services (AWS) Cloudfront
- ► Adding memcached to a Rails application
- ► Adding Redis to a Rails application
- ► Implementing low-level caching in Rails
- ► Caching rendered views
- ► Aborting long requests with Rack::Timeout
- ► Using a follower for read-only DB queries

Introduction

Fast applications drive more user engagement and a better experience. Every developer wants their application to be highly responsive. Also, with the proliferation of mobile devices on slower connections, we need to be more focused than ever on web performance.

But how do we do it? There is no single trick to have a fast application. It takes time and a combination of different techniques to reduce our page load time. We must attack the problem from different angles and optimize each layer within our applications stack. In this chapter, you will learn how to optimize a Ruby on Rails application. You'll learn about asset optimization, caching, and a few tricks that are specific to Heroku.

Setting up a sample blogging app

In this recipe, we will set up a simple blogging application that we'll use throughout the rest of the chapter. It's a simple Rails application that has had no performance enhancements. With each recipe in this chapter, you'll learn different ways to make it faster.

 Completed code samples for each recipe are available in the separate branches of the project's GitHub repository at https://github.com/ mscoutermarsh/blogger-app.

How to do it...

Here, we will get the example application up and running on your local machine. We'll then deploy it to Heroku. Let's begin by opening up a terminal using the following steps:

1. First, we'll need to get a copy of the source code by cloning the Git repository:

    ```
    $ git clone https://github.com/mscoutermarsh/blogger-app.git
    ```

2. Next, let's navigate to the new directory and install the application's gems:

    ```
    $ cd blogger-app
    $ bundle install
    ```

     This application uses a Postgres database; if you do not already have Postgres installed on your machine, you'll need to make sure that it's set up before continuing.

3. Next, we'll need to set up the application's database and run migrations. We can do this with the following `rake` commands:

    ```
    $ bundle exec rake db:create
    $ bundle exec rake db:migrate
    ```

4. This application has some seed data to prepopulate your database; let's run it now:

    ```
    $ bundle exec rake db:seed
    ```

5. Now, let's start up the application:

    ```
    $ bundle exec rails s
    ```

6. If we open a browser and navigate to `http://localhost:3000`, we'll be able to see the Blogger app running.

7. Now that we have our application running locally, let's deploy it to Heroku. First, we'll need to create a new application:

```
$ heroku create
```

 We can optionally include an app name after `create`. If not, Heroku will autogenerate one for us with the `$ heroku create app-name` command.

8. To deploy, push the master branch to Heroku:

```
$ git push heroku master
```

9. Now that we've pushed our code, we'll need to run migrations and seed the database:

```
$ heroku run rake db:migrate
$ heroku run rake db:seed
```

 Heroku will autodetect that our application uses Postgres and will set up a hobby-level database for us.

10. All that's left now is to open up our application to see it running:

```
$ heroku open
```

See also

▸ Take a look at the GitHub repository for the Blogger app at `https://github.com/mscoutermarsh/blogger-app`

Using Heroku Deflater to gzip assets

One of the quickest ways to increase web performance is to enable GNU Zip (gzip) for our assets. It's a file compression format that can reduce the size of our HTML, CSS, and JavaScript assets by up to 70 percent. It only takes a couple of minutes to be enabled. In this recipe, you'll learn how this can be done.

Getting ready

Before adding gzip to our application, it can be interesting to run a benchmark so that we can compare our application before and after the change.

We can do this in our browser with YSlow. For installation instructions, visit `https://developer.yahoo.com/yslow/`.

Once installed, we can run a test and then click on **Statistics** to see a pie chart that shows our page weight.

Running this before and after will show what a huge impact gzip has on web performance.

How to do it...

All we need is one additional gem to start serving the gzipped assets on Heroku. Open a terminal and navigate to our example application, the Blogger app, by performing the following steps:

1. Open our Gemfile and add the following line:

   ```
   gem 'heroku-deflater', group: :production
   ```

2. Now, run `bundle install`, commit our changes, and push them to Heroku:

   ```
   $ bundle install
   $ git commit -am 'Installing Heroku deflater to GZip assets'
   $ git push heroku master
   ```

3. That's it! To finish up, let's open up our app and rerun the YSlow test. We will see a drastic difference:

   ```
   $ heroku open
   ```

How it works...

For the example Blogger application, here are the before and after results from YSlow. Enabling gzip resulted in a 73 percent improvement!

Before:

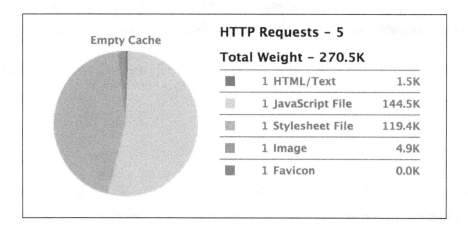

After:

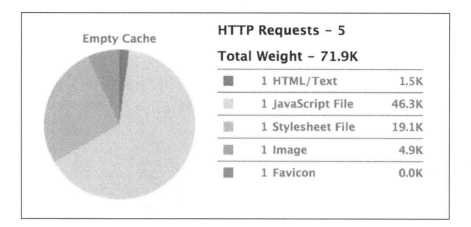

The Heroku Deflater gem adds additional Rack middleware to our Rails application. When the request for an asset comes into our application, the middleware will look for a gzipped version of the asset. If it's available, it will serve it to the user.

If our application is using the asset pipeline, we are pretty much guaranteed to have the gzipped assets available. During the precompile process, the asset pipeline automatically creates gzipped versions for us.

See also

▸ The example source code for this recipe is available at `https://github.com/mscoutermarsh/blogger-app/tree/gzip_assets`

▸ To learn more about how gzip works, visit `https://developers.google.com/speed/articles/gzip`

▸ The Heroku Deflater gem at `https://github.com/romanbsd/heroku-deflater`

Serving assets from Amazon Web Services (AWS) Cloudfront

We can drastically reduce the number of requests to our dynos by having all the static assets of our application served by a **Content Delivery Network** (**CDN**). Static assets are the images, CSS, and JavaScript used by our application. Using a CDN is a huge performance win for any application. It helps us by freeing up our dynos from serving static assets, and it also gets our assets to our users' machines faster.

In this recipe, you will learn how to take an existing Rails application and have its assets served by AWS Cloudfront for speedy delivery to users.

Getting ready

For this recipe, we will need an AWS CloudFront account.

Visit `http://aws.amazon.com/cloudfront/` to sign up now. Alternatively, if you have an existing AWS account, you can sign in.

How to do it...

We'll need to set up a CloudFront distribution and make a few minor changes to our Rails application. Let's get started by opening a browser and configuring CloudFront first, using the following steps:

1. We'll need to open up the CloudFront dashboard and create a new distribution to use with our Heroku application. We can do this by visiting `https://console.aws.amazon.com/cloudfront/home` and clicking on **Create Distribution**.

2. On the next screen, we'll select **Web** for our delivery method.

3. Now, we will configure our CloudFront distribution by entering the URL of our Heroku application and giving it a name (**Origin ID**). If our application supports SSL (HTTPS), we should select **Match Viewer** for **Origin Protocol Policy**; otherwise, we can leave it set to **HTTP Only**. This is shown in the following screenshot:

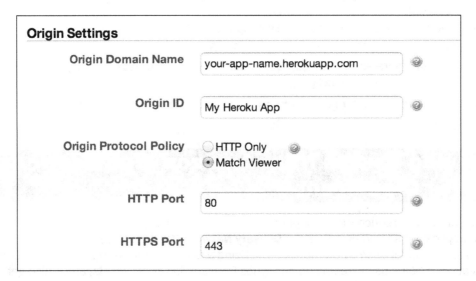

If our application has a custom domain name, we should use this here for **Origin Domain Name**.

4. Let's ensure that we take note of the **Price Class** setting. This determines where our content is served. The closer it is to our users, the faster it will be for them to download it.

Distribution Settings

Price Class | Use All Edge Locations (Best Perform ♦ | ◎

 It's best to have **Price Class** set to **Use All Edge Locations**. However, if our application is only used in a specific area, we can save some money by having our content hosted only on a more limited number of servers. For pricing information, visit `http://aws.amazon.com/cloudfront/pricing/`.

5. We can leave the rest of the settings to CloudFront's defaults. We're now ready to click on **Create Distribution**, and our CDN will be ready to be set up. It might take a few minutes until it is ready to use. Take note of the distribution's **Domain Name**; we will be using this in the next step.

6. Now that CloudFront is set up for us, we need to configure our Rails application to use it. We can do this by adjusting a few settings.

7. Let's open up `config/environments/production.rb` in our Rails project. We need to set our asset host to our new CloudFront distribution's domain. We can do this by adding the following line to our production config. We'll use an environment variable here to make it easily configurable through Heroku:

```
config.action_controller.asset_host =
  ENV['CLOUDFRONT_URL']
```

 By adding this to `production.rb`, our application will only use CloudFront when deployed to Heroku and when our `RAILS_ENV` configuration variable is set to production.

8. Now, we can add our CloudFront domain name to our Heroku application's configuration settings. We will get this value from the CloudFront dashboard:

```
$ heroku config:set CLOUDFRONT_URL=//example-url.cloudfront.net
```

Notice that the domain starts with //. This allows our assets to load over either HTTP or HTTPS. If our application only uses one or the other, we can specify it in the configuration variable.

9. To finish up, all that's left is to commit our changes and push them up to Heroku:

```
$ git commit -am 'Adding Cloudfront to production config'
$ git push heroku master
$ heroku open
```

 We do not have to upload our assets to CloudFront. It works by pulling our assets directly from our servers when the users request them.

10. If we watch our logs, we'll see that our application will stop receiving requests to serve static assets. They are now being served from CloudFront instead of our dynos:

```
$ heroku logs --tail
```

How it works...

When a user makes a request to our web application, it must travel from wherever the user is located to our server. This works great for users who are located near our application's data center. However, for users who are further away, the additional travel time for each request can make our application less responsive. CloudFront has a network of servers throughout the world that cache our application's static assets. Then, when a user loads our application, CloudFront responds to the request from the nearest location. This makes our application considerably faster by reducing network latency and the load on our dynos.

 Worried about serving stale assets? Rails' asset pipeline protects us from serving the wrong version by adding a unique fingerprint to each CSS and JS file. Whenever there is a change, the new file will be distributed to CloudFront, ensuring that our users always get the correct version.

See also

▶ Refer to the example source code for this recipe available at https://github.com/mscoutermarsh/blogger-app/tree/cloud_front

▶ As an alternative to CDN, we can use CloudFlare available at https://www.cloudflare.com

▶ AWS CloudFront is available at http://aws.amazon.com/cloudfront/

▸ Rails Asset Pipeline is available at `http://guides.rubyonrails.org/asset_pipeline.html`

Adding memcached to a Rails application

Memcached is a high-performance, distributed, key-value store that allows us to quickly store and retrieve data from memory. It helps us scale our web applications by storing the result of any expensive operations in memory. A common use case is storing the result of a database query in memcached. Then, the query only has to be made once; the subsequent requests for that data are loaded from memcached. This reduces the load on our database and makes our application significantly faster. We can use memcached to cache database calls, API requests, and even the rendered views. In this recipe, you'll learn how to get a Rails application up and running with memcached on Heroku.

 If we are new to implementing caching, memcached should be our first choice. It's rock solid and easy to use. There are many other caching options available, but memcached is the standard.

Getting ready...

We'll run memcached on our local development machine to test it.

On OS X, we can quickly install it using Homebrew:

```
$ brew install memcached
```

On Ubuntu, we can use `apt-get`:

```
$ apt-get install memcached
```

For directions specific to other operating systems, take a look at memcached's wiki at `https://code.google.com/p/memcached/wiki/NewInstallFromPackage` for up-to-date instructions.

How to do it...

To set up memcached on Rails, we'll need to add two gems to our project and make a couple of configuration changes to our application using the following steps:

1. We'll start by adding the `dalli` and `memcachier` gems. Let's add the following lines to our Gemfile and then run `bundle install`:

```
gem 'memcachier'
gem 'dalli'
```

```
$ bundle install
```

2. Now, we need to tell Rails to use memcached in production. Open up your `config/environments/production.rb` file and set `cache_store` to use Dalli with the following line:

```
config.cache_store = :dalli_store, nil, {expires_in: 1.day,
compress: true}
```

The second argument is typically the address of the memcached server. Here, we are leaving it set to `nil` because the MemCachier gem will set up our connection for us using environment variables. We are also able to set default options for the connection; here we set all cache keys to expire after 24 hours, and we also enabled compression for large objects.

 By default, Rails will use an in-memory store in development, unless we specifically tell it to use memcached.

3. We might also want to run memcached in development; this can be useful when testing and debugging caching issues. To do this, we'll add the following line to our `config/environments/development.rb` file:

```
config.cache_store :dalli_store
```

We can leave it without any arguments; Dalli will find and connect to our local memcached server automatically.

 For caching to work in development mode, we'll have to enable it. We can do this by setting `config.action_controller.perform_caching` to `true`. It's best not to check this change into the repository; it can be confusing for other developers when the application caches unexpectedly.

4. We'll now need to enable a memcached add-on for our Heroku application. MemCachier has a developer tier server that we can try for free. Let's add it now by running the following command:

```
$ heroku addons:add memcachier
```

5. Now, if we take a look at our configuration variables, we'll see that the MemCachier add-on has added three variables. These will be used by our application to connect to memcached:

```
$ heroku config
MEMCACHIER_PASSWORD:      05c6bf08xx
MEMCACHIER_SERVERS:       mc1.xxx.ec2.memcachier.com:11211
MEMCACHIER_USERNAME:      e34dxx
```

6. To finish up, let's commit and push our changes to Heroku:

```
$ git add .
$ git commit -m 'Setting up memcached'
$ git push heroku master
```

7. We can test out reading and writing values from a Rails console with the following commands:

```
$ heroku run rails c
$ Rails.cache.write('test', 123)
$ Rails.cache.read('test')
=> 123
```

 We can clear memcached at any time by running $ `Rails. cache.clear` from a Rails console.

How it works...

The Dalli gem manages the connection between Ruby and our memcached server. We used the MemCachier gem simply for convenience. It allows Dalli to connect to MemCachier on Heroku without making any configuration changes. It simply uses the environment variables provided by the MemCachier add-on to make the connection.

It's easiest to think of memcached as a super-powered hash. It's a key-value store that we can use to temporarily store any data that our application needs. It's a distributed cache; this means that it can run across multiple servers, and it will distribute our data evenly across them. If one server fails, we will only lose access to some of our data. The other servers will be available to pick up the slack, and our application will regenerate any missing data.

With the MemCachier add-on, our data is automatically spread across multiple memcached servers. We simply need to choose how much memory we need, and MemCachier takes care of the rest.

See also

▶ Setting up memcached is just the beginning. For ways to take full advantage of it, check out the *Implementing low-level caching in Rails* and *Caching rendered views* recipes that are explained later in this chapter.

▶ The full example source code for this recipe is available at `https://github.com/ mscoutermarsh/blogger-app/tree/memcached`.

- ▶ To know more about the Dalli gem, visit `https://github.com/mperham/dalli`.
- ▶ To know more about MemCachier, visit `https://www.memcachier.com/`.

Adding Redis to a Rails application

Redis is a high-performance, in-memory, key-value store with persistence. It's a great alternative to memcached for caching, with the additional functionality of a NoSQL data store. Here, we will learn how to add Redis to our application and set it up to be used as a cache.

Getting ready...

We'll first set up a Redis server on our development machine using the following steps:

1. Let's start by installing Redis.

    On OS X, we can use Homebrew to install Redis with the following command:

    ```
    $ brew install redis
    ```

    For Ubuntu, we can use `apt-get`:

    ```
    $ sudo apt-get update
    $ sudo apt-get install redis-server
    ```

    For other operating systems, we can get installation instructions from the Redis website (`http://redis.io/download`).

2. Once installed, we can verify that our installation is working by trying out a couple of commands. Redis comes with a command-line program, `redis-cli`.

    Let's start it up and try setting and getting a key/value pair:

    ```
    $ redis-cli
    $ set testing 123
    OK
    $ get testing
    "123"
    ```

 Check out the Redis website for a full listing of all the commands. Each command is usable in `redis-cli`. Visit `http://redis.io/commands` for more information.

How to do it...

Now that we have Redis running on our local machine, we can add it to our Rails application using the following steps:

1. Let's start by opening up our Gemfile and adding the `redis` and `redis-rails` gems:

    gem 'redis'

    gem 'redis-rails'

2. Now, install the gems:

    $ bundle install

3. We'll need to create a new initializer for Redis at `config/initializers/redis.rb` and add the following code:

    ```
    if ENV['REDISTOGO_URL']
      uri = URI.parse(ENV['REDISTOGO_URL'])
      Redis.current = Redis.new(host: uri.host, port: uri.port,
    password: uri.password)
    else
      Redis.current = Redis.new
    end

    REDIS = Redis.current
    ```

4. Now, let's configure production to use Redis for caching. We can do this by opening up `config/environments/production.rb` and adding the following line. If we have an existing cache store setting, we'll need to replace it:

    ```
    config.cache_store = :redis_store, "#{ENV["REDISTOGO_URL"]}/0/
    cache", {expires_in: 24.hours}
    ```

5. For development, we can optionally use Redis caching as well. To do this, we can add the following code to `config/environments/development.rb`:

    ```
    config.cache_store = :redis_store, "redis://localhost:6379/1/
    cache", {expires_in: 24.hours}
    ```

For caching to work in development mode, we'll have to enable it. We can do this by setting `config.action_controller.perform_caching` to `true`. It's best to not check this change into the repository; it can be confusing for other developers when the application caches unexpectedly.

6. To check whether Redis is working properly, we can open up a Rails console and try out a couple of commands:

```
$ bundle exec rails c
$ REDIS.set('testing', 123)
=> "OK"
$ REDIS.get('testing')
=> "123"
```

7. Now, we'll need to add the Redis To Go add-on to our Heroku application:

```
$ heroku addons:add redistogo
```

 For more information on the available plans, visit `https://addons.heroku.com/redistogo`.

8. To finish up, we'll need to commit our changes and push them up to Heroku:

```
$ git add .
$ git commit -m 'Setting up Redis'
$ git push heroku master
```

How it works...

Redis is a strong alternative to using memcached for caching in a Rails application. The primary difference between the two is that Redis persists our data to disk and also allows us to use more complex data structures (such as ordered sets and lists). The ability to store more complex data objects makes Redis a popular choice in applications that require any persisted queuing or sorting.

If caching queries and views is the extent of our need, then memcached is a great choice. If we need a NoSQL datastore as well, Redis will cover both needs. Conveniently, in a Rails application, both Redis and memcached are interchangeable for caching. If you start out using memcached for caching and later switch to Redis, the change is simple to make.

See also

▶ To take full advantage of Redis caching, check out the *Implementing low-level Rails caching* and *Caching rendered views* recipes later in this chapter.

▶ Refer to the example source code for this recipe available at `https://github.com/mscoutermarsh/blogger-app/tree/redis`

▶ Learn more about Redis by visiting `http://redis.io`.

- ▶ Learn more about Redis To Go available by visiting `http://redistogo.com`.
- ▶ Learn more about the Redis Rails gem by visiting `https://github.com/redis-store/redis-rails`

Implementing low-level caching in Rails

We can significantly increase the performance of our application by caching queries to our database. In Rails, this is known as **low-level caching**. In this recipe, you will learn how to use `Rails.cache.fetch` to cache database queries. You'll see that this technique can be used to cache any expensive operations. Any outside API or network calls also make great candidates for low-level caching. We will be able to use this technique to make significant performance improvements to our application. We'll reduce the load on our database as well as speed up our overall response times.

Getting ready

To complete this recipe, our Rails application needs to have either Redis or memcached set up. For us to test cache in development, we will also need to have it enabled in our development config.

Let's open up `config/environments/development.rb` now and ensure that we have the following line set to `true`:

```
config.action_controller.perform_caching = true
```

How to do it...

Let's get started with caching by trying it out in a Rails console using the following steps:

1. Open up a console and run a normal ActiveRecord count query:

```
$ bundle exec rails c
$ Post.count
 (0.3ms)  SELECT COUNT(*) FROM "posts"
=> 2
```

2. Now, let's run this query again, but this time let's use the `fetch` method to cache the result:

```
$ Rails.cache.fetch('post_count'){ Post.count }
 (0.4ms)  SELECT COUNT(*) FROM "posts"
=> 2
```

3. If we run the same code again, we'll see that this time it does not run the query. It pulls the result from the cache and returns it:

```
$ Rails.cache.fetch('post_count'){Post.count}
=> 2
```

 Don't believe it? Restart the Rails console and run it again. The value will still be cached.

4. We can create a new post and see that when using `fetch`, the count will not update because it is cached:

```
$ Post.create(title: 'New post!', content: 'Heroku!', author:
Author.first)
$ Post.count
   (0.5ms)   SELECT COUNT(*) FROM "posts"
=> 4
```

If you try the cache again, you'll notice that it remains the same:

```
$ Rails.cache.fetch('post_count'){Post.count}
=> 2
```

5. Now, let's cache something a little more useful. In the Blogger example app, we have an index page that displays all our posts. However, since it isn't updated often, we would like to cache it to reduce the number of queries to our database. In `app/controllers/posts_controller.rb`, we have the following action:

```
def index
  @posts = Post.all
end
```

To cache this query for 1 hour, you can change it to the following:

```
def index
 @posts = Rails.cache.fetch('all posts',
                               expires_in: 1.hour){Post.all}
end
```

6. Our index page will now load much faster but can potentially have stale data, as the posts will only be loaded once an hour. This is a trade off we must consider when implementing any caching. If we want to clear the "all posts" cache before it expires, we can use the `delete` method:

```
Rails.cache.delete('all posts')
```

How it works...

Let's dig a little deeper into how the `Rails.cache.fetch` method works:

```
fetch(cache_key, options = nil) { block }
```

The `fetch` method will check our cache using `cache_key`. If it finds data, it will return the value. If there is no data for this key, it will run whatever block of code we passed to it. The result of this code will then be returned and stored in our cache for future requests.

> For multiline code blocks, we should use do/end. The last line in the block will be the return value:
>
> ```
> Rails.cache.fetch 'posts with categories' do
>   tucker = Author.find_by_name('Tucker')
>   posts = Post.includes(:categories)
>   posts.where(author: tucker)
> end
> ```

The `fetch` method can also accept a variety of options. One of the most useful options is `expires_in`. This sets the number of seconds until the cache key expires. If we do not pass an expiration value, `fetch` will use the default `expires_in` setting that we have in our `config/environments/production.rb` file.

Another useful option is `race_condition_ttl`. It's an important setting for blocks of code that receive a high volume of requests. It protects our application from what's commonly known as **stampeding** or **dog piling**. This is when multiple requests all reach an expired cache that's in the process of being regenerated. This causes the cache to be regenerated by each request; this can be dangerous in high-traffic situations if the code is a particularly expensive operation. We only need the cache to be regenerated once by a single request. We can avoid stampeding by setting `race_condition_ttl`. When the first request sees that the cache has expired, it will increase the expiration of the current cache key by the number of seconds specified by `race_condition_ttl`. This will keep the other processes from trying to update the cache and will give the first process time to update it.

> If we ever need to invalidate a cache key, we can use `Rails.cache.delete(cache_key)`.

See also

▶ The example source code for this recipe available is at `https://github.com/mscoutermarsh/blogger-app/tree/cache_queries`

▶ The Rails Cache Store documentation is available at `http://api.rubyonrails.org/classes/ActiveSupport/Cache/Store.html`

Caching rendered views

Rendering a page in Rails isn't a simple process. It usually consists of several database queries that render various partials and convert HAML to HTML. Repeating this entire process for each page load is wasteful. In this recipe, you will learn how to cache your views so that you only have to render them once. You'll also learn how to use key-based cache expiration to ensure that you're always serving the latest content.

How to do it...

In this recipe, we'll use the Blogger application as an example to implement view caching. This time, we will optimize `posts#show` using caching to make viewing a post as fast as possible.

 Make sure that caching is enabled in `config/environments/development.rb` and `config.action_controller.perform_caching` is set to `true`.

1. Currently, if we try to view a post, our application does the following to render the page:

```
Started GET "/posts/2" for 127.0.0.1 at 2014-08-09 14:29:06 -0400
Processing by PostsController#show as HTML
  Parameters: {"id"=>"2"}
  Post Load (0.4ms)  SELECT  "posts".* FROM "posts"  WHERE
"posts"."id" = $1 LIMIT 1  [["id", 2]]
  Author Load (0.8ms)  SELECT  "authors".* FROM "authors"  WHERE
"authors"."id" = $1 LIMIT 1  [["id", 1]]
  Rendered authors/_author.html.erb (0.1ms)
   (0.9ms)  SELECT COUNT(*) FROM "categories" INNER JOIN
"categories_posts" ON "categories"."id" = "categories_
posts"."category_id" WHERE "categories_posts"."post_id" = $1
[["post_id", 2]]
```

```
  (0.2ms)   SELECT "categories"."name" FROM "categories" INNER
JOIN "categories_posts" ON "categories"."id" = "categories_
posts"."category_id" WHERE "categories_posts"."post_id" = $1
[["post_id", 2]]
  Rendered posts/_categories.html.erb (7.1ms)

  Rendered posts/show.html.erb within layouts/application (19.5ms)

  Rendered layouts/_navigation_links.html.erb (0.3ms)

  Rendered layouts/_navigation.html.erb (0.9ms)

  Rendered layouts/_messages.html.erb (0.0ms)
Completed 200 OK in 32ms (Views: 23.3ms | ActiveRecord: 6.8ms)
```

This view has been kept simple for example purposes. We can see from the log that it executes four queries and renders five partials. It took 32 ms to render this page; let's see how much we can improve this using caching.

 As this is a simple application, the uncached response time is already fast. The same techniques can be applied to more complex views.

2. Let's start by adding caching to the two partials used to render the post. We can do this by wrapping them in `cache` blocks.

   In `app/views/authors/_author.html.erb`, modify the code as follows:

```erb
<% cache author do %>
  <p>
    <strong>Author:</strong>
    <%= author.name %>
  </p>
<% end %>
```

   Then, in `app/views/posts/_categories.html.erb`, modify the code as follows:

```erb
<% cache categories do %>
  <strong>
    <%= 'Category'.pluralize(categories.count) %>:
  </strong>
  <%= categories.pluck(:name).join(', ') %>
<% end %>
```

Now, if we refresh the page a couple of times, we'll see in the logs where it writes to the cache and on subsequent requests from which it reads the cache. We reduced our page load time to 18 ms and now run only three queries instead of four:

```
Started GET "/posts/2" for 127.0.0.1 at 2014-08-09 14:50:48 -0400
Processing by PostsController#show as HTML
  Parameters: {"id"=>"2"}
  Post Load (0.3ms)  SELECT  "posts".* FROM "posts"  WHERE
"posts"."id" = $1 LIMIT 1  [["id", 2]]
  Author Load (0.2ms)  SELECT  "authors".* FROM "authors"  WHERE
"authors"."id" = $1 LIMIT 1  [["id", 1]]
  Cache digest for app/views/authors/_author.html.erb:
2d15ca308dec9cb981ee3ee47e6ae58e
Read fragment views/authors/1-20140803035250466666000/2d15ca308dec
9cb981ee3ee47e6ae58e (0.2ms)
  Rendered authors/_author.html.erb (1.0ms)
  Cache digest for app/views/posts/_categories.html.erb:
2eb832c69061fa6e6e4fb75bcab52f8f
  Category Load (0.4ms)  SELECT "categories".* FROM "categories"
INNER JOIN "categories_posts" ON "categories"."id" = "categories_
posts"."category_id" WHERE "categories_posts"."post_id" = $1
[["post_id", 2]]
Read fragment views/categories/1-20140803035250393298000/
categories/2-20140803035250459525000/2eb832c69061fa6e6e4fb75bcab52
f8f (0.2ms)
  Rendered posts/_categories.html.erb (3.0ms)
  Rendered posts/show.html.erb within layouts/application (7.2ms)
  Rendered layouts/_navigation_links.html.erb (0.3ms)
  Rendered layouts/_navigation.html.erb (0.8ms)
  Rendered layouts/_messages.html.erb (0.0ms)
Completed 200 OK in 19ms (Views: 16.9ms | ActiveRecord: 0.9ms)
```

In our logs, we can see the cache key used by Rails. If we want, we can see the exact HTML that was cached by opening a Rails console and using `Rails.cache.read('cache key here')` to see the value for this key.

3. This is a great start; by going one step further and adding caching to the posts/show view, we'll create this page even faster. Let's do this now:

In `app/views/posts/show.html.erb`, modify the code as follows:

```erb
<p id="notice"><%= notice %></p>
<% cache @post do %>
  <p>
    <strong>Title:</strong>
    <%= @post.title %>
  </p>

  <p>
    <strong>Content:</strong>
    <%= @post.content %>
  </p>

  <p>
    <%= render @post.author %>
  </p>

  <p>
    <%= render partial: 'categories', locals: {categories: @post.
categories} %>
  </p>

  <%= link_to 'Edit', edit_post_path(@post) %> |
  <%= link_to 'Back', posts_path %>
<% end %>
```

4. Now, if we watch our logs and refresh the page a couple of times, we'll see new data being written to our cache and then read back:

```
Started GET "/posts/2" for 127.0.0.1 at 2014-08-09 15:10:48 -0400
Processing by PostsController#show as HTML
  Parameters: {"id"=>"2"}
  Post Load (0.2ms)  SELECT "posts".* FROM "posts"  WHERE
"posts"."id" = $1 LIMIT 1  [["id", 2]]
  Cache digest for app/views/authors/_author.html.erb:
2d15ca308dec9cb981ee3ee47e6ae58e
```

```
    Cache digest for app/views/posts/_categories.html.erb:
    2eb832c69061fa6e6e4fb75bcab52f8f

    Cache digest for app/views/posts/show.html.erb:
    d7c63a8ae84971db73176d172b51391e

Read fragment views/posts/2-20140803035250546865000/
d7c63a8ae84971db73176d172b51391e (0.1ms)

    Rendered posts/show.html.erb within layouts/application (2.2ms)

    Rendered layouts/_navigation_links.html.erb (0.3ms)

    Rendered layouts/_navigation.html.erb (1.2ms)

    Rendered layouts/_messages.html.erb (0.0ms)

Completed 200 OK in 15ms (Views: 13.5ms | ActiveRecord: 0.2ms)
```

5. We now reduced the page load to 15 ms; this is more than a 50 percent improvement over our original page. We can also see that the page is now only executing a single query.

 If we like, we can even cache the remaining query using `Rails.cache.fetch` in the `posts#show` controller action.

How it works...

Now that we have the post, author, and categories all being cached for this page, what will happen if one of them gets updated? We wouldn't want our users to be viewing stale content. Rails takes care of this for us by basing the cache key on the `updated_at` attribute for the object it is caching. This means each time a post is updated, a new cache key will be used for the content:

```
views/posts/2-20140803035250546865000/d7c63a8ae84971db73176d172b51391e
        ^class ^id ^updated_at              ^template digest
```

One tricky part of using `updated_at` in our cache keys is that it does not account for changes made in the associated models. If we update a child model, it will not bump its parent's `updated_at` field as well by default.

There are two solutions to this problem. For `belongs_to` associations, we can use the `touch: true` option. When this option is set on a `belongs_to` association, whenever the child is updated, it will also update the parent object's `updated_at` field effectively, refreshing the parent's cache key:

```
belongs_to :author, touch: true
```

The second solution is to include the associated object in the cache key. We can do this by passing an array with each of the objects to the `cache` method. For example, in the Blogger app, you might want to include both the associated author and categories in the cache key. So, if either is updated, the cache for the post will be regenerated:

```
<% cache [@post, @post.author, @post.categories] do %>
  # content here
<% end %>
```

Using a separate cache block for each object in our view allows us to take advantage of a concept known as **Russian Doll caching**. In the `posts#show` example, we have a cache block around the entire post and then others around the author and categories. If we update only the post, the author and category caches will remain intact and will be used when regenerating the cache for the entire post. This makes rendering more efficient, because we only have to regenerate the caches that changed rather than everything.

The final piece of the cache key to be aware of is the template digest. This is the value at the end of the cache key and is a fingerprint of our view template. This ensures that if any code in our view is changed, the cache key will no longer be valid, and it won't serve the old view code.

Managing cache invalidation through cache keys can create a large number of unused cache objects. When backed by memcached, this is fine, because if memcached runs out of memory, it will replace the oldest unused objects with new objects. If our caching backend is Redis, we need to make sure that we have an expiration set for all our cache keys; otherwise, our memory usage can expand very quickly.

See also

▶ The example source code for this recipe is available at `https://github.com/mscoutermarsh/blogger-app/tree/cache_views`

▶ Learn more about how the cache key is generated at `http://api.rubyonrails.org/classes/ActiveSupport/Cache.html#method-i-expand_cache_key`

▶ Refer to David Heinemeier Hansson's post at `http://signalvnoise.com/posts/3113-how-key-based-cache-expiration-works` to understand how key-based cache expiration works

Aborting long requests with Rack::Timeout

A pile up of long running requests is a sure way to bring our entire application to a screaming halt. When a web request to a Heroku application takes longer than 30 seconds to respond, Heroku will terminate the request and return an H12 error to the user. The problem with this is that this does not actually stop the request from being processed by our dynos. Even though the user will never receive a response, our dynos will keep working on the request until it is complete. This is an obvious waste of resources, but we can easily avoid this by adding Rack::Timeout to our applications.

How to do it...

To set up Rack::Timeout, we'll need to add a gem to our Gemfile and an initializer to our Rails app. Let's fire up a terminal and navigate to our `blogger-app` directory by performing the following steps:

1. We can start by adding `rack-timeout` to our Gemfile:

   ```
   gem 'rack-timeout'
   ```

2. Then, install the gem by running `bundle install`:

   $ bundle install

3. Now, we'll need to add a new initializer at `config/initializers/timeout.rb` with the following code:

   ```
   Rails.application.middleware.use Rack::Timeout
   Rack::Timeout.timeout = 10  # seconds
   ```

    This will time out any requests that take over 10 seconds. We should tune this for our individual application; 10 seconds might be too aggressive for some apps.

4. All that's left is to commit our changes to Git and push them to Heroku:

   ```
   $ git add .
   $ git commit -m 'Adding timeout for long running requests'
   $ git push heroku master
   ```

How it works...

When Heroku receives a request at its router, it adds an X-Request-Start header to the request. This header contains the time that the request was received by Heroku. The `Rack::Timeout` middleware that we installed in this recipe uses the header to determine how long a request has been running. As the request is processing, it will periodically check whether it has exceeded the timeout period. If it has gone on for too long, Rack::Timeout will throw `RequestTimeoutError` and end the request.

Aborting requests is something that should happen very rarely. It's essentially a safety valve to protect our dynos from doing unnecessary work. There is no point in continuing to process a request if it will never get back to the user.

Rack::Timeout is useful in situations where our users have found some edge case in our application that performs slowly. When they do not get a response back quickly, they keep refreshing the page, sending more slow requests into our application to be processed.

Aborting requests is something that will be used very rarely. It's for cases where our application is overwhelmed or users have found a way of using our application that is destructive. It protects us from long-running requests that steal resources away from our application's normal requests. If we see our application regularly serving slow requests, we should optimize them as quickly as possible. Slow requests can lead to larger problems, as they tie up resources that other requests are using.

See also

- The example source code for this recipe is available at `https://github.com/mscoutermarsh/blogger-app/tree/rack_timeout`
- To learn more about Rack::Timeout, visit `https://github.com/heroku/rack-timeout`

Using a follower for read-only DB queries

As an application grows, the database is typically one of the largest performance bottlenecks. The first step in horizontally scaling a database is to enable replication to a follower database. When we enable a Postgres follower, all writes to the master database are streamed to the follower. This gives us a read-only replica of all our data. We can then reduce the load on our primary database by directing read-only queries to a follower database. This frees up resources on our master database to handle writes.

Replication lag is the delay between the write to the primary database and this data's availability on the follower. We need to be aware that there might occasionally be a second delay before the data is on the follower.

Getting ready

First, we'll need to set up a follower database on Heroku. For instructions on how to do this, refer to the *Creating a read-only follower* recipe in *Chapter 9, Using and Administrating Heroku Postgres*.

 Follower databases are only available on standard or higher database tiers.

How to do it...

To take advantage of our follower database, we'll need to set up the Octopus gem in our Rails application. It will manage the read-only connection for us by performing the following steps:

1. First, let's open up our Gemfile and add `ar-octopus`:

    ```
    gem 'ar-octopus'
    ```

2. Next, let's install it by running `bundle install`.

    ```
    $ bundle install
    ```

3. Now, we'll need to set up a configuration file that tells Octopus how to connect to our follower database. It creates a connection called `read_only` that we'll be able use in our application. Let's create a new file, `config/shards.yml`, and paste in the following code. We'll need to adjust the settings so that they match what's in our application's existing `config/database.yml` file.

     This is only for development and testing. It sets our `read_only` follower to point at our primary database. We'll use an initializer to configure production.

    Have a look at the following code:

    ```
    octopus:
      replicated: true
      fully_replicated: false
      development:
        read_only:
    ```

```
      adapter: postgresql
      encoding: unicode
      database: blogger-postgres_development
      pool: 5
      username: postgres
      password:
  test:
    read_only:
      adapter: postgresql
      encoding: unicode
      database: blogger-postgres_test
      pool: 5
      username: postgres
      password:
```

 This file is also available on GitHub at `https://github.com/ mscoutermarsh/blogger-app/blob/follower_db/config/ shards.yml`.

4. At this point, we will be able to test Octopus by running a query against our `read_ only` database. Let's open up a Rails console and try it out:

   $ bundle exec rails c

   $ Octopus.using(:read_only) { Post.first }

   We can use `Octopus.using` to specify the follower database. We can then pass a block to the method to execute any ActiveRecord calls. In this example, we used the `read_only` follower to load the first record of the posts table.

 Having trouble? Double-check whether the `shards.yml` configuration matches your `database.yml` file for testing and development. Make sure that the follower is named `read_only` as shown in the preceding example.

5. We're now ready to set up Octopus in production. For this, we'll create a new initializer at `config/initializers/octopus.rb`. We're using an initializer so that we can control our follower database using a Heroku configuration variable. If we use a configuration variable in `shards.yml`, it will get messy quickly. Using an initializer is a cleaner solution:

   ```
   # config/initializers/octopus.rb
   # Uses FOLLOWER_DATABASE_URL
   # to configure a follower DB for octopus
   ```

```ruby
require 'uri'

if %w{production staging}.include? Rails.env
  follower_url = ENV['FOLLOWER_DATABASE_URL']

  begin
    url = URI.parse(follower_url)
  rescue URI::InvalidURIError
    raise "Invalid FOLLOWER_DATABASE_URL"
  end

  Octopus.setup do |config|
    config.environments = [:production, :staging]
    config.shards = {read_only:
                       {adapter: 'postgresql',
                        database: url.path.split('/').last,
                        username: url.user,
                        host: url.host,
                        port: url.port,
                        password: url.password}
    }
  end
end
```

 This file is also available on GitHub at `https://github.com/ mscoutermarsh/blogger-app/blob/follower_db/config/ initializers/octopus.rb`.

6. Since we're using Unicorn for this application, we'll need to configure Unicorn to make the additional database connections when starting up. Let's change our `config/ unicorn.rb` file to match the following code. The changes specific to Octopus are highlighted in the following code:

```ruby
worker_processes Integer(ENV['WEB_CONCURRENCY'] || 3)

# kill long running requests. Default: 15 seconds
# Heroku's default is 30 seconds.
timeout Integer(ENV['WEB_TIMEOUT'] || 15)
preload_app true

before_fork do |server, worker|

  Signal.trap 'TERM' do
```

```
    puts 'Unicorn master intercepting TERM and sending myself QUIT
  instead'
    Process.kill 'QUIT', Process.pid
  end

  if defined?(ActiveRecord::Base)
      shards = ActiveRecord::Base.connection_proxy.instance_
  variable_get(:@shards)

    shards.each do |shard, connection_pool|
      connection_pool.disconnect!
    end

    ActiveRecord::Base.connection.disconnect!
  end
end

after_fork do |server, worker|

  Signal.trap 'TERM' do
    puts 'Unicorn worker intercepting TERM and doing nothing. Wait
  for master to sent QUIT'
  end

  Octopus.config['production']['master'] = ActiveRecord::Base.
connection.config
    ActiveRecord::Base.connection.initialize_shards(Octopus.config)
end
```

 This `unicorn.rb` file is also available on GitHub at `https://github.com/mscoutermarsh/blogger-app/blob/follower_db/config/unicorn.rb`.

7. The Octopus initializer uses a configuration variable, FOLLOWER_DATABASE_URL, to set up the read_only connection. Next, we'll need to set this variable in our application to the value of our follower's DATABASE_URL variable. Let's first take a look at our available Postgres databases; we'll see that there is an entry for our follower DB. We'll know which database is our follower, because it will have a line that shows what DB it is following:

$ heroku pg

=== HEROKU_POSTGRESQL_GREEN_URL

Plan: Standard Yanari

Status:	Available
Data Size:	6.6 MB
Tables:	5
PG Version:	9.3.4
Connections:	5
Fork/Follow:	Unavailable on followers
Rollback:	earliest from 2014-08-03 16:05 UTC
Created:	2014-08-02 17:38 UTC
Data Encryption:	In Use
Following:	HEROKU_POSTGRESQL_CHARCOAL
Behind By:	0 commits
Maintenance:	not required

Now that we know which DB is our follower, let's grab its `database_url` from our configuration settings. We'll pass the DB name we found in the previous step to the next command:

```
$ heroku config:get HEROKU_POSTGRESQL_GREEN_URL
```

It will return a value like this:

```
postgres://a:b@ec2-00-235-69-000.compute-1.amazonaws.com:5792/
g3d7fe
```

Let's take that value and add `FOLLOWER_DATABASE_URL` to it:

```
$ heroku config:set FOLLOWER_DATABASE_URL=postgres://a:b@ec2-00-
235-69-000.compute-1.amazonaws.com:5792/g3d7fe
```

 If we're missing the `FOLLOWER_DATABASE_URL` configuration variable, our application will not start in production.

8. We've now finished setting up Octopus; let's commit our changes and push them to Heroku:

```
$ git add .
$ git commit -m 'Setting up a read-only follower with Octopus'
$ git push heroku master
```

Using the follower database

Now that our follower database is set up, let's learn how to make use of it using the following steps:

1. A good place to start is with any queries for the data that isn't updated often or won't cause problems if it's up to a second behind the primary database.

    In the Blogger app, a good example of this is the index page for posts. In `app/controllers/posts_controller.rb`, we can see that the index action loads all of the posts. We can have it use the follower database for this query by wrapping the ActiveRecord call in `Octopus.using`:

    ```
    def index
      @posts = Octopus.using(:read_only) { Post.all }
    end
    ```

    Now, whenever a user visits our `Posts#index` page, the query used to grab all of the posts will run against our follower DB.

2. We can also direct all the reads for specific models to the follower database. Octopus has a `replicated_model` method that we can use in our models. This will force all writes to go to the primary database and all reads to use the follower.

    In the Blogger app, a good candidate for this is the `Category` model. It isn't written too often but receives a lot of reads:

    ```
    class Category < ActiveRecord::Base
      replicated_model
      has_and_belongs_to_many :posts
      validates_presence_of :name
    end
    ```

How it works...

The first step in horizontally scaling an application's database is to set up a follower and begin moving reads to it. This allows us to reduce the load on our primary database and free up more resources for writes. We need to carefully consider each query that we set up to use our follower. As queries are executed on the primary database, they are streamed to the follower database. This keeps the follower in sync with the primary database at all times. The delay between the primary and follower will vary based on the volume of queries being run. Under normal circumstances, changes will be synced within a few milliseconds.

Another benefit of having a follower database is that in the event that our primary fails, we can quickly failover to the follower. The follower will become the new primary database and will be ready to take over the load, because it has been in sync all the time. This saves us the time of instantiating another database and restoring a backup of our data. The failover can happen in a matter of seconds rather than minutes or hours (depending on how quick we are).

The `octopus.rb` initializer that we used in this recipe is a little different than the conventional usage of `shards.yml` for the production Octopus configuration. As your goal here was to configure a single follower database, using an initializer was the simpler (and more readable) solution. It allows us to follow the Heroku convention of using a configuration variable for our database connections. It is possible to do this with `shards.yml`, but we will have to mix both Ruby and YAML in the same file to do it correctly.

See also

- The full example source code for this recipe is available at `https://github.com/mscoutermarsh/blogger-app/tree/follower_db`
- To learn more about Octopus, visit its page on GitHub at `https://github.com/tchandy/octopus`
- Refer to Heroku's Postgres documentation on using followers at `https://devcenter.heroku.com/articles/heroku-postgres-follower-databases`

9

Using and Administrating Heroku Postgres

In this chapter, we will cover the following recipes:

- ▶ Creating and sizing a new database
- ▶ Promoting a Heroku database
- ▶ Connecting to Heroku Postgres from Navicat
- ▶ Connecting to Heroku Postgres from psql
- ▶ Creating a database backup
- ▶ Restoring from a backup
- ▶ Creating a read-only follower
- ▶ Viewing and stopping database processes
- ▶ Analyzing Heroku Postgres's performance

Introduction

With Heroku Postgres, most of the pain of administering a database has been automated, giving us more time to focus on building and growing our applications. Security, health checks, scaling, backup, and recovery have all been simplified for us.

Your database is one of the most crucial pieces of your application's infrastructure. Its performance and security are of top priority when running a production-level application. In this chapter, you will be introduced to using Postgres the Heroku way. You'll start by learning how to select the correct database plan for your application. Once you have your database, you'll learn how to administer it, manage backups, and monitor performance, all via the Heroku CLI.

Creating and sizing a new database

You're ready to set up a new Postgres database on Heroku. But how do you decide which plan is right for your situation? In this recipe, you will determine what database size and plan you will need for a new Heroku application. Rather than guessing, you can take some simple steps to properly size your database from the start.

How to do it...

When selecting a database, there are several choices we need to make to ensure we are on the right plan. We'll need to determine uptime requirements, as well as data size and how many connections our application needs. Once we have this information, it is rather easy to determine which plan is right for our application.

Selecting a tier

The first decision we need to make in choosing a database is picking which database tier our application needs:

1. Heroku has four database tiers: hobby, standard, premium, and enterprise. For any production-level application, we have to be at least on the standard tier. Hobby tier databases are only meant for testing the platform and basic development.

2. Uptime is the primary consideration we need to be making when choosing a database tier. While downtime cannot be predicted, if something occurs that affects our database, on the standard tier, we could see up to a maximum of 1 hour of downtime per month. The premium tier guarantees a maximum of 15 minutes.

 Premium tier databases have a stand-by database ready and waiting for automatic failover if something ever goes wrong.

If high availability is important to our application, we should choose a premium or enterprise-level plan.

Determining data size

The second step in choosing a database is determining how much RAM our database needs. We can do this by finding out how much memory it takes to store all our data. Ideally, we want our database to have enough RAM to store all of its data in memory:

1. If we have an existing database with Heroku, we can determine its data size with the `pg:info` command:

    ```
    $ heroku pg:info
    ```

    If we have an existing Postgres DB on another provider, we can find the data size by running the following command in psql:

    ```
    \l+
    ```

     That's a lowercase L in the preceding command.

2. Once we have the data size, it's up to us to make a rough estimate of how much our data might grow. We should choose a plan with more RAM than data. If our data size is 350 MB, then a plan with 1 GB of RAM will be a good fit. As our application grows, we can always upgrade to a larger database instance as needed.

Connection limits

Each plan has a limited number of available connections that our application can use. You can calculate how many connections your application needs fairly easily:

1. To see how many connections your application is currently using, you can run the following command:

    ```
    $ heroku pg:info
    === HEROKU_POSTGRESQL_GRAY_URL  (DATABASE_URL)
    Plan:        Hobby-dev
    Status:      Available
    Connections: 4
    PG Version:  9.3.3
    Created:     2014-07-27 21:01 UTC
    ```

2. The number of database connections will depend on what language/framework our application is developed in. We'll typically see one database connection per application process or thread. If we're using a multiprocess server such as Unicorn, we can count on using one connection per Unicorn worker that we're running. If we are running three workers on each dyno and have five dynos, our application needs a minimum of 15 available connections to run.

3. We must also account for any connections that our worker processes will be using and should give ourselves plenty of room for growth. When we're scaling up to quickly handle increased load on our application, the last thing we want to worry about is running out of database connections and having to upgrade our database.

Selecting and creating the database

Now that we understand our criteria to select a database plan, we can go ahead and pick one. We now know how much data we currently use, the level of uptime we require, and the number of connections our application needs. Armed with this information, selecting a plan is much simpler.

To finish up, let's head over to `https://addons.heroku.com/heroku-postgresql`. From here, we can select our database and either create it through the web interface or copy the command provided and run it in a terminal.

How it works...

In the preceding steps, you picked a plan with more RAM than the total data in your database. The reasoning behind this is that you want a cache hit rate of as close to 100 percent as possible. This means that when your application queries your database, whatever data it needs should be available in RAM, making it very quick to retrieve. If you have more data than the available RAM and your application queries for it, then Postgres will have to use the hard drive to access the data. This is significantly slower and counts as a **cache miss**. If you can afford a database plan large enough for this, you should absolutely do it. Your application's performance and users will be glad you did.

See also

▸ Read more about Postgres's performance and cache hit rate in this excellent blog post by Craig Kerstiens at `http://www.craigkerstiens.com/2012/10/01/understanding-postgres-performance/`

Promoting a Heroku database

In your applications, you should be using the `DATABASE_URL` configuration variable to connect to your database. It's not an uncommon occurrence, especially when upgrading a database to have multiple databases for a single application. Heroku makes it easy for us to manage which database's credentials are assigned to `DATABASE_URL` through a process known as **promotion**. At any time, you can promote any database assigned to your application and make it primary by updating `DATABASE_URL`. This makes it simple to swap databases without any risk of pasting incorrect credentials.

How to do it...

To start, let's open up a terminal and take a look at our current configuration variables:

1. Let's run `heroku config` to view our existing settings:

    ```
    $ heroku config
    DATABASE_URL: postgres://user:password@ec2-54-221-206-165.
    compute-1.amazonaws.com:5432/d8hg98vjvtisu4

    HEROKU_POSTGRESQL_GRAY_URL: postgres://user:password@ec2-54-235-
    69-186.compute-1.amazonaws.com:5792/d75vuqlr37fe

    HEROKU_POSTGRESQL_ORANGE_URL: postgres://user:password@ec2-54-221-
    206-165.compute-1.amazonaws.com:5432/d8hg98vjvtisu4
    ```

2. In this example, we can see that we have two different databases from our configuration variable: HEROKU_POSTGRESQL_GRAY and HEROKU_POSTGRESQL_ORANGE. Currently, DATABASE_URL is set to credentials for the ORANGE database.

    If we want to change this and have the GRAY database be our primary, we can use `promote` to quickly update DATABASE_URL.

3. Let's promote the GRAY database to be our primary one using the `pg:promote` command:

    ```
    $ heroku pg:promote HEROKU_POSTGRESQL_GRAY
    Promoting HEROKU_POSTGRESQL_GRAY_URL (DATABASE_URL) to DATABASE_
    URL... done
    ```

4. Now that the new DATABASE_URL variable is set, we'll want to restart our application so that it starts using the new settings:

    ```
    $ heroku restart
    ```

5. Once our dynos restart, our application will be using our recently promoted database.

How it works...

It's always good practice to keep your configuration settings separate from your application's source code by using environment variables in Heroku. PG promote is simply a convenience method to manage your different databases in an easier way. You'll find that you use it often when upgrading or changing database plans.

Connecting to Heroku Postgres from Navicat

Navicat is a popular GUI for database administration. In this recipe, you will learn how to set up a connection to your Heroku Postgres database in Navicat.

Getting ready

To start, you'll first need to download and install Navicat. For this recipe, you'll need a version of Navicat that is compatible with Postgres.

You can either use **Navicat for Postgres** or you can use **Navicat Essentials**. The essentials version is a less-expensive edition of Navicat with a limited feature set aimed at more basic database administration tasks.

The download and installation instructions are available here:

▶ Navicat for Postgres at `http://www.navicat.com/products/navicat-for-postgresql`

▶ Navicat Essentials at `http://www.navicat.com/products/navicat-essentials`

How to do it...

Once we have Navicat installed, we'll need to set up a connection to our Heroku Postgres database:

1. Let's start by getting the credentials for our Heroku database. We can do this by looking at our `DATABASE_URL` configuration variable.

    We can also get these credentials from the Heroku Postgres dashboard at `https://postgres.heroku.com/databases`.

   Let's run the following command:

   ```
   $ heroku config:get DATABASE_URL
   postgres://username:password@ec2-55-221-206-165.compute-1.
   amazonaws.com:5432/dXhg98vjvtisu4
   ```

2. The string returned to us by the previous command contains everything we need to connect to our Postgres database. If we're not familiar with this URL format, it can be a little confusing. Let's break it down:

   ```
   postgres://username:password@host:port/database_name
   ```

3. Now that we have our credentials, let's open up Navicat and click on the
    Connection icon in the top-left corner:

4. Let's start filling in our credentials by using what we retrieved in the previous steps.
    For a database URL that looks like this:

    ```
    postgres://username:password@ec2-55-221-206-165.compute-1.
    amazonaws.com:5432/dXhg98vjvtisu4
    ```

    We'd fill in the following:

    - **Connection Name**: We will add our application name as `Heroku Postgres`
    - **Host Name/IP Address**: This will be `ec2-55-221-206-165.compute-1.amazonaws.com`
    - **Port**: The port number will be `5432`
    - **Default Database**: This will be `dXhg98vjvtisu4`
    - **User Name**: The username has to be entered in this field
    - **Password**: The password has to be entered in this field

5. Next, we'll need to click on the **SSL** button and make sure **Use SSL** is checked. Once checked, we can test our connection by clicking on **Test Connection**:

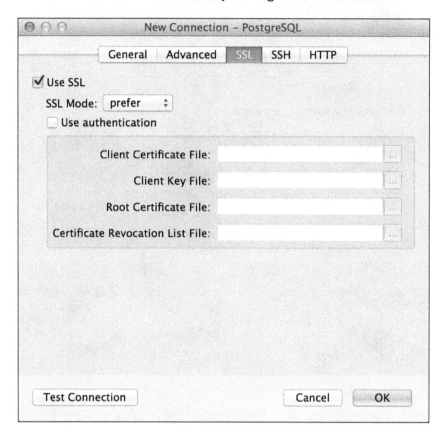

6. To finish up, we can click on **OK** and begin using Navicat with our Postgres database.

 Having trouble connecting? Make sure that each field is correct and that **Use SSL** is checked.

How it works...

Navicat is a great administration tool that makes it easy for us to view and work with our data. Heroku Postgres allows us to connect to our database from anywhere as long as we are over a secure connection (SSL). Other database administration tools will have similar setups, and you can use what you learned here to connect to your database with them as well.

See also

▶ Check out OxDBE as an alternative to Navicat at `http://www.jetbrains.com/dbe/`

▶ For MySQL databases, take a look at SequelPro available at `http://www.sequelpro.com/`

Connecting to Heroku Postgres from psql

Psql is the terminal application that ships with Postgres. It enables us to run queries and administer our Postgres databases from the command line. With Heroku, you can either use the Heroku CLI to start up a psql session or you can connect to your database using only psql. In this recipe, you'll be introduced to both methods.

How to do it...

To start, let's open up a terminal:

1. We can quickly start up a psql session through the Heroku CLI by running the `pg:psql` command:

   ```
   $ heroku pg:psql
   ```

    To exit the psql session, type `\q` and hit *Enter* or press *Ctrl + D*.

2. By default, it will connect to the database in our `DATABASE_URL` config variable. If we want to connect to a different database, we need to specify the name:

   ```
   $ heroku pg:psql ORANGE
   ```

3. We don't have to use the Heroku CLI to connect to our database. If we'd like, we can use plain psql from the command line. We can get our credentials from the `DATABASE_URL` configuration variable, and then pass them to the `psql` command:

   ```
   $ PGPASSWORD=pass psql -U user -h host.com -p 5432 -d database-name
   ```

 Remember, the `DATABASE_URL` variable is formatted as `postgres://username:password@host:port/database_name`.

How it works...

Psql does not accept a password as an argument. You can instead set an environment variable on your machine with your password, PGPASSWORD. Without setting this variable, psql will prompt us for the password on login. If you'd like, you can store all of your database login information in a .pgpass file in your home directory.

You can do this by creating a file and setting its permissions to only be accessible by the user:

```
$ touch ~/.pgpass && chmod 0600 ~/.pgpass
```

You can then place your credentials in the file in each line in the following format:

```
hostname:port:database:username:password
```

 Although this is rare, your Heroku Postgres credentials can change at any time. If your database host fails and Heroku needs to move your database, the credentials you have saved will no longer be valid. Heroku will always keep your DATABASE_URL variable up to date with the latest credentials.

See also

To learn more about connecting to psql, refer to the documentation on the password file available at http://www.postgresql.org/docs/9.3/static/libpq-pgpass.html

Creating a database backup

In case disaster strikes, you should always have a recent backup of your database that is somewhere accessible and easy to restore from so that you can get back up and running quickly. In this recipe, you will learn how to have Heroku automatically back up data for you. You'll also learn how to manually create backups and store them away from Heroku for extra peace of mind.

How to do it...

To begin, we'll need to open up a terminal and navigate to our Heroku application:

1. We can enable database backups with the Heroku add-on PG Backups. There are three different backup options, and they are all free. The best option does daily backups and retains our data for up to one month. Let's install that now:

    ```
    $ heroku addons:add pgbackups:auto-month
    ```

To see the other plans, take a look at the PG Backups add-on (`https://addons.heroku.com/pgbackups`).

2. Now that the add-on is installed, we can use it to capture a backup of our database:

```
$ heroku pgbackups:capture
HEROKU_POSTGRESQL_GRAY_URL (DATABASE_URL)  ----backup--->  b001

Capturing... done
Storing... done
```

 By default, `capture` will back up the database in our DATABASE_URL configuration variable. If we'd like to back up a different database, we can pass it as an argument by using the `$ heroku pgbackups:capture HEROKU_POSTGRESQL_ORANGE_URL` command.

3. We can view all of our backups by running `pgbackups` with no arguments. We'll see that each backup has its own ID; these will come in handy later:

```
$ heroku pgbackups
ID     Backup Time
----   ------------------------
b001   2014/08/24 14:56.26 +0000
b002   2014/08/24 15:03.59 +0000
```

4. If we'd like to download a backup, we can create a URL to download it from with the `url` command:

```
$ heroku pgbackups:url b002
```

This command will return a URL that we can use to download our backup.

If we want to do all of this from the command line in a single command, we could combine the command with cURL. This will save the backup to `dbbackup.dump`:

```
$ curl -o dbbackup.dump `heroku pgbackups:url b002`
```

How it works...

The `pgbackups` add-on is a convenient way for us to create backups from the Heroku CLI. It's identical to using Postgres's `pg_dump` utility. The Heroku add-on takes care of running the dump and storing it for us daily.

Since it uses `pg_dump`, the backup file created can be transferred easily to any other Postgres database (whether on Heroku or not). This makes it fairly easy for us to switch providers if we ever need to. We're not locked into using only Heroku Postgres for our database needs.

See also

▶ To learn more about `pg_dump`, take a look at its documentation on Postgres's website at `http://www.postgresql.org/docs/9.3/static/app-pgdump.html`

Restoring from a backup

A backup of your database is useless unless you are able to quickly and reliably restore from it. This process is something that you won't use often, but it's critical that you know how to do it and have practiced using it. If you ever need to do an emergency restore, you want to be confident that you can and know how to do it. In this recipe, you will be learning how to recreate your database on Heroku from a Postgres dump.

Getting ready

You'll need to have the `pgbackups` add-on installed and a backup of your database created. For instructions on how to do this, refer to the previous recipe, *Creating a database backup*.

How to do it...

To start, let's open up a terminal. We'll be using the Heroku CLI to restore our backup:

1. To restore our primary database from our most recent backup, we can run the `pgbackups:restore` command without any arguments:

   ```
   $ heroku pgbackups:restore
   ```

   It will take the most recently created backup and restore it to the database set in our `DATABASE_URL`.

    Remember, we can always see a list of our available backups on Heroku by running `$ heroku pgbackups`.

2. If we want, we can specify the database we want to restore to, as well as the specific backup ID:

   ```
   $ heroku pgbackups:restore HEROKU_POSTGRESQL_GRAY_URL b001
   ```

3. We do not have to use a backup that is only on Heroku. If we have a `.dump` file somewhere that is accessible on the Internet, we can give Heroku the URL and it will download and use it to restore our database:

```
$ heroku pgbackups:restore HEROKU_POSTGRESQL_GRAY_URL 'https://
s3.amazonaws.com/example-url/backup.dump'
```

 S3 works great in storing database dumps. Make sure to remove the dump from being publically accessible after the restore is complete.

How it works...

Postgres has a `pg_restore` utility to restore from backups. Heroku has wrapped its functionality nicely in the `pgbackups:restore` command, making it easy for us to recover our database from a backup. The `restore` command is destructive and the state your database was in before the restore operation will not be recoverable. If you're nervous at all about attempting to restore your database, you can always create a new database, do the restore, and then use `promote` to replace your existing database.

See also

▶ To learn more about how `pg_restore` works, take a look at its documentation on the PostgreSQL website (`http://www.postgresql.org/docs/9.3/static/app-pgrestore.html`)

Creating a read-only follower

Follower databases can be used to create redundancy, scaling, or upgrading your existing database. Once a follower is set up, all data written to the primary database will be synced over to the follower. In this recipe, you will learn how to quickly get a follower set up and synced with your primary database.

 Primary/follower databases are also commonly referred to as master/slave. On Heroku and in this book, we'll be using the terms primary and follower.

How to do it...

We'll be setting up our follower database using the Heroku dashboard.

Followers can only be created for Standard or Premium databases. We'll need to upgrade if we are using a development or hobby-level database. To see if followers are available on our database, we can run $ `heroku pg`.

We will perform the following steps:

1. Let's open a browser and go to `https://postgres.heroku.com/databases` and click on our application's primary database.

2. Next, we'll click on the gear icon in the top-right corner and then add **Follower Database**:

3. We'll need to pick a database size for our follower; we should use the same size as our existing primary database. Once we click on **Create**, our follower will be created and data from the primary database will start syncing. We can check on its status with the `pg:wait` command:

```
$ heroku pg:wait

Waiting for database HEROKU_POSTGRESQL_ORANGE_URL... \ preparing
(37% completed)
```

4. The wait time will depend on the size of our primary database. Once finished, we'll see that Heroku has added a configuration variable to our application that we can use to connect to our follower.

How it works...

Heroku Postgres is great at making normally complex tasks very simple. Being able to quickly set up a follower database is a huge asset to us as your application grows.

Redundancy

The added redundancy of having a follower will allow us to quickly recover from any failure in our primary database. Using the `pg:unfollow` command, we can convert any follower into a primary database. Since it has been kept in sync with the existing primary, its data is already up to date and ready to go. Followers are also created on different infrastructures than their primary. This protects us by distributing our data across multiple datacenters, significantly reducing our risk in the event that there is a failure.

> Premium and enterprise Heroku Postgres plans come with a follower for high availability failover. They will automatically failover in the event that the primary fails.

Horizontal scaling

Adding a follower is one of the first steps in scaling a database. With some changes to your application, you can begin distributing reads to your follower database. This reduces the number of queries against your primary database, giving it more resources to handle writes. Any long running queries (such as business intelligence/reporting) can be directed to the read-only follower. This isolates your application from any decrease in performance due to any infrequent but resource-intensive queries.

See also

- ▶ Refer to the Postgres wiki to learn more about replication at `https://wiki.postgresql.org/wiki/Replication,_Clustering,_and_Connection_Pooling`
- ▶ Take a look at the *Using a follower for read-only DB queries* recipe in *Chapter 8, Optimizing a Rails Application on Heroku*, to learn how to use a follower in a Rails application

Viewing and stopping database processes

One option to diagnose database performance issues is by looking at the database's currently running processes. This will give us insight into exactly what is taking up resources and potentially causing problems. In this recipe, you will be learning how to use the Heroku CLI to view and stop processes running on your database.

How to do it...

To begin, let's open up a terminal; we'll be using the Heroku CLI in this recipe:

1. To view the currently running processes on our database, we can use the `pg:ps` command. We'll see an output of what is currently running. Each process has its own unique ID (PID, or process ID):

    ```
    $ heroku pg:ps
    pid | state |      source     | running_for |
    ----+-------+-----------------+-------------
    343 | active | /app/bin/rails | 00:04:23.0286
    ```

     This example has been condensed for readability.

2. In this example, we have a query that has been running for over 4 minutes. We can stop this query with the `pg:kill` command. We use the `pid` found from the previous command and pass it to `pg:kill` to stop the process from running:

    ```
    $ heroku pg:kill 343
    ```

     If our database is in a really bad condition, we can kill every running process by using the `$ heroku pg:killall` command.

How it works...

Postgres has a table, `pg_stat_activity` that contains all of its currently running processes. Heroku has created commands in its CLI to nicely wrap and present the data available in this table. If you're curious to see the raw data Heroku is working with, you can query `pg_stat_activity` directly:

```
SELECT * FROM pg_stat_activity where datname = 'our-heroku-db-name';
```

If we're ever in a situation where our database performance is suffering for unknown reasons, checking the currently running processes is a quick way to find the cause. Also, if needed, you can take action and end the offending process.

See also

▶ To learn more about the statistics that Postgres monitors, take a look at Postgres's documentation available at `http://www.postgresql.org/docs/9.3/static/monitoring-stats.html`

Analyzing Heroku Postgres's performance

Database performance is critical to have a highly responsive web application. Heroku gives us a handful of tools to analyze our Postgres database for performance issues. Knowledge is power, and having visibility into emerging issues can help us fix them before they turn into major problems. In this recipe, you will learn about your cache hit rate, slow queries, and unused indexes.

Getting ready

In this recipe, we will be making use of the `pg-extras` plugin for Heroku. It gives us access to additional commands to administer our Postgres database.

To install it, you need to open a terminal and run the following command:

```
$ heroku plugins:install git://github.com/heroku/heroku-pg-extras.git
```

How to do it...

We'll be using the Heroku CLI to monitor the performance of our database.

1. To get an overview of our database's general health, we can run the `pg:diagnose` command:

```
$ heroku pg:diagnose
GREEN: Connection Count
GREEN: Long Queries
GREEN: Idle in Transaction
GREEN: Indexes
GREEN: Bloat
GREEN: Hit Rate
GREEN: Blocking Queries
GREEN: Load
```

It quickly does eight different health checks on our database and reports back any issues that it finds. If any of the checks are red, we'll receive suggestions on how to fix them or find more information.

2. Having a cache hit rate as close to 100 percent as possible is critical for a database that responds to queries quickly. We can see what our cache hit rate is by using the `pg-extras cache-hit` command:

```
$ heroku pg:cache-hit
      name      |        ratio
----------------+-----------------------
 index hit rate | 0.99922477136372828798
 table hit rate | 0.99936977126404112551
(2 rows)
```

Each of these ratios show how often our database retrieves data from memory (cache) rather than having to go to the hard disk. If we ever see a number lower than 98 percent, we should consider upgrading our database size so that more of our dataset can live in memory. Queries that are served directly from cache are magnitudes faster than those that require reading from disk.

 To see all of the `pg-extras` available commands, run
`$ heroku pg --help`.

3. Indexes can take up a lot of memory, so we should make sure that they are worth the overhead and are being used. We can see how often they are used with the `pg:index-usage` command:

```
$ heroku pg:index-usage
       relname       | percent_of_times_index_used | rows_in_table
---------------------+-----------------------------+---------------
 categories_posts    |                             |         44063
 posts               | 99                          |         22012
 authors             | 0                           |         13137
 schema_migrations   | Insufficient data           |             2
 categories          | 99                          |             2
(5 rows)
```

In this example, we can see that this table never uses its index.

For further details, we can use the `pg:unused-indexes` command:

```
$ heroku pg:unused-indexes
      table      |          index          | index_size | index_scans
-----------------+-------------------------+------------+------------
 public.authors  | index_authors_on_name   | 784 kB     |           0
(1 row)
```

Now, it's clear exactly which index is never used and how much space it is taking up. This specific index only uses 784 kilobytes of RAM, which is pretty insignificant. If we wanted, we could remove it to free up some memory.

4. Finally, the last thing we should check when monitoring our database's performance is for any slow queries. There are multiple ways we can do this.

   For extremely slow queries that have been running for over 5 minutes, we can use the `pg:long-running-queries` command:

   ```
   $ heroku pg:long-running-queries
   ```

   To see our application's top 10 slowest queries, we can run `pg:outliers`:

   ```
   $ heroku pg:outliers
   ```

 It's good practice to regularly look at our slowest queries. If we can make it a habit of optimizing them, our database's performance will improve.

If we'd like to view our slowest queries from the Web, we can do that as well by going to `https://postgres.heroku.com`, navigating to our database, and then scrolling down. Our expensive queries are listed on the dashboard, as shown in the following screenshot:

```
Expensive queries

This shows queries ranked by their frequency (throughput). These queries are the most important to optimize, as they occur frequently.
You should aim to have frequent queries execute in under 10 ms. Read more about how.

   Most time consuming    Slowest execution time    Highest throughput    Slowest I/O                                    ⏱ Last week ▾

        33%       1 ms       86/min       0ms    INSERT INTO "posts" ("author_id", "content", "created_at", "title",
    Time cons.   Avg. time   Throughput   I/O time  "updated_at") VALUES ($1, $2, $3, $4, $5) RETURNING "id"


        33%       1 ms       13/min       0ms    SELECT "posts".* FROM "posts" WHERE "posts"."id" = $1 LIMIT ?
    Time cons.   Avg. time   Throughput   I/O time
```

How it works...

All of the information gathered by `pg-extras` comes from the various stats tables in Postgres. You can see the exact queries that each of these commands run against your database by viewing the source code of the `pg-extras` plugin.

Here's the source: `https://github.com/heroku/heroku-pg-extras/blob/master/lib/heroku/command/pg.rb`.

With this information, you can do regular checkups of your database and uncover issues at an early stage. Monitoring these different metrics as your application grows will help you in planning upgrades and optimizing your application's code for best performance.

See also

- ▸ The `pg-extras` plugin at `https://github.com/heroku/heroku-pg-extras`
- ▸ To learn about Postgres's statistics tables, check out the documentation at `http://www.postgresql.org/docs/9.3/static/monitoring-stats.html`

10
The Heroku Platform API

In this chapter, we will cover:

- ▶ Making our first API request with HTTPie
- ▶ Getting started with the Platform API gem
- ▶ Scaling dynos and workers
- ▶ Managing configuration variables
- ▶ Adding and removing collaborators
- ▶ Creating new Heroku applications

Introduction

As developers, we love APIs. They give us the power to build anything we want with our favorite services. Heroku's Platform API gives us full control over our Heroku applications, allowing us to automate and script to our heart's content.

In this chapter, we'll be introduced to the basics of making a request to the Heroku API. We'll then move on to learn some of the more advanced features and how we can use them in real-world situations. By the end of this chapter, we'll have the information we need to write our own scripts to manage our Heroku applications.

Making our first API request with HTTPie

The Heroku Platform API is a set of HTTP endpoints that enables us to fully manage our applications. Each endpoint has a set of available actions. They are RESTful; this means that they use HTTP request types (GET, PATCH, POST, and DELETE) to determine what action we want from the API. GET is used to retrieve data such as a list of our applications. PATCH is used to make updates to the existing data, such as making a change to a configuration variable. POST is used to create something new, such as a new application. Finally, DELETE is used for exactly what it sounds like, deleting data.

In this recipe, we will learn about the conventions to make requests to the Heroku API. We will also be introduced to HTTPie, which is a command-line tool to send HTTP requests. It's similar to cURL, but easier to use.

Getting ready

To begin, we'll need to install HTTPie on our machine.

OS X

On OS X, we can install HTTPie via Homebrew:

```
$ brew install httpie
```

Linux

Depending on our flavor of Linux, there are HTTPie packages available via `apt-get`:

```
$ apt-get install httpie
```

They are also available via `yum`:

```
$ yum install httpie
```

Windows

For Windows, we can install HTTPie via Pip (`https://pip.pypa.io`):

```
$ pip install httpie
```

> Having trouble with installation? Visit HTTPie on GitHub at `https://github.com/jakubroztocil/httpie` for more information.

How to do it...

For our first request, we will use HTTPie to get a JSON version of the Platform API schema. This request does not require any form of authentication. It makes for a good first attempt at using the API.

 All Heroku API requests must be done over HTTPS.

Let's perform the following steps:

1. For each API request, we need to include an Accept header. This specifies which version of the API we are trying to access. To start, let's try sending a request without an Accept header to see what happens:

```
$ http https://api.heroku.com/schema
HTTP/1.1 404 Not Found
Cache-Control: no-transform
Connection: keep-alive
Content-Length: 168
Content-Type: text/plain
Date: Sat, 06 Sep 2014 13:04:57 GMT
Request-Id: bcfa2ec6-67d3-48a2-aae4-d0f10a1250bc
Server: nginx/1.4.7
Status: 404 Not Found
X-Cascade: pass
X-Content-Type-Options: nosniff
X-Runtime: 0.007322096
```

```
The requested API endpoint was not found. Are you using the
right HTTP verb (i.e. `GET` vs. `POST`), and did you specify your
intended version with the `Accept` header?
```

We received a 404 error because we did not specify an Accept header in the request.

 We can add -v to any HTTPie command to see a verbose output.

2. If we try the request again with the Accept header set correctly, we'll receive a response. Let's try this now:

```
$ http https://api.heroku.com/schema
Accept:'application/vnd.heroku+json; version=3'

HTTP/1.1 200 OK

Cache-Control: public, max-age=3600

Connection: keep-alive

Content-Encoding: gzip

Content-Type: application/schema+json

Date: Sat, 06 Sep 2014 13:15:22 GMT

RateLimit-Remaining: 2399

Request-Id: d6ab5428-c2ae-4d5f-ae18-ed67b1e8fd03

Server: nginx/1.4.7

Status: 200 OK
```

This request returned a status of 200, as well as a listing of each endpoint and action available on the Heroku Platform API.

> Having trouble with the Accept header? Make sure it is surrounded by single quotes in the HTTP command, application/vnd.heroku+json; version=3

3. Now that we've successfully made our first request, let's learn how to make an authenticated request. First, we'll need to get our API token. We can do this from the Heroku CLI with the following command:

```
$ heroku auth:token

4f39171e-2e0c-432d-9282-99x59a315312
```

4. Now that we have our token, let's use it to view information about our account:

```
$ http https://api.heroku.com/account
        Accept:'application/vnd.heroku+json; version=3'
        -a :'4f39171e-2e0c-432d-9282-99x59a315312'
        HTTP/1.1 200 OK
Connection: keep-alive

Content-Encoding: gzip

Content-Length: 232

Content-Type: application/json;charset=utf-8

Date: Sat, 06 Sep 2014 22:39:42 GMT

ETag: "efeafb4cc0a048c2f1809ca63d9bce33"
```

```
Last-Modified: Thu, 04 Sep 2014 00:17:37 GMT

Oauth-Scope: global

Oauth-Scope-Accepted: global identity

RateLimit-Remaining: 2392

Request-Id: 7f9d8be7-2ebb-4845-8d0f-9f6323e01ba8

Server: nginx/1.4.7

Status: 200 OK

Vary: Accept-Encoding

X-Content-Type-Options: nosniff

X-Runtime: 0.044324164
```

```
{
    "allow_tracking": true,
    "beta": false,
    "created_at": "2010-02-03T03:34:45Z",
    "email": "Coutermarsh.mike@gmail.com",
    "id": "xxx212b3-960c-4dbf-b7bf-008d7e8310e6",
    "last_login": "2014-09-04T00:17:37Z",
    "name": "Mike Coutermarsh",
    "two_factor_authentication": false,
    "updated_at": "2014-09-04T00:17:37Z",
    "verified": true
}
```

 Having trouble? In the previous command, be sure to pass the authentication in the -a : 'token' format. This tells HTTPie to use basic authentication, with no username, and our token as the password. The token will be converted to the base64 format before being sent.

5. We now know the basics of making a request to the Heroku API. To see a full listing of all the available endpoints, we can view the complete documentation at https://devcenter.heroku.com/articles/platform-api-reference.

How it works...

Now, we are able to make simple authenticated requests to the Heroku API using HTTPie. The basics that we learned here will also apply to any other method of making requests to the Heroku API. We will always need to include an Accept header, and for authenticated requests, we'll need to use HTTP basic authentication with our API token.

Having to add authentication to each HTTPie request can be a little tedious. Luckily, we can easily avoid this if we authenticate the Heroku Toolbelt. When we log in with the Heroku CLI, using `$ heroku auth:login`, Heroku adds an entry to our machine's `~/.netrc` file that contains our API token. This is what allows us to continue using the CLI without logging in each time. HTTPie is already set up to be compatible with netrc. Before sending each request, HTTPie checks our `~/.netrc` file, and if it sees credentials for the requested URL (`api.heroku.com`), it will automatically include them in the request.

See also

- To learn more about REST, take a look at the introductory tutorial at `http://code.tutsplus.com/tutorials/a-beginners-guide-to-http-and-rest--net-16340`

- HTTPie on GitHub at `https://github.com/jakubroztocil/httpie`

- CLI authentication with netrc at `https://devcenter.heroku.com/articles/authentication`

- For a simple GUI HTTP client, try Postman at `http://www.getpostman.com/`

Getting started with the Platform API gem

Heroku has created a Ruby gem that makes it easy for us to take full advantage of the Platform API from Ruby. In this recipe, we'll learn how to get up and running with the gem and on our way to integrating the Heroku API with our own Ruby applications. We'll also be introduced to Pry, a super-powerful Ruby shell to execute and explore code. It will help us get up to speed and learn the Heroku API gem quickly.

Getting ready

To start, let's download some sample code to get familiar with the Platform API gem.

1. Let's open up a terminal and use Git to clone the sample code:

   ```
   $ git clone https://github.com/mscoutermarsh/heroku-api-examples.git
   $ cd heroku-api-examples
   ```

2. We'll need Ruby 2.1.2 to run these examples. If we have RVM installed, we can select 2.1.2:

   ```
   $ rvm use 2.1.2
   ```

    If it isn't installed, RVM will give us instructions on how to install it.

3. Now, let's install the dependencies by running bundler:

```
$ bundle install
```

How to do it...

We now have everything we need to get started with the Heroku Platform API gem.

1. The first thing we'll want to do is try making an authenticated request to the API. In the `heroku-api-examples` repository we set up earlier, let's take a look at `authentication.rb`:

```
require 'platform-api'

heroku_api = PlatformAPI.connect_oauth('your_token_here')

puts heroku_api.account.info
```

The purpose of this file is to see whether we can successfully authenticate and make a request to the Heroku API.

 Notice that we require `'platform-api'` at the beginning of this file. We need to do this because it's a plain Ruby file. This isn't needed in a Rails application because Rails will automatically load it for us.

2. Let's replace `your_token_here` in `authentication.rb` with our Heroku API token. We can get it by running the following command:

```
$ heroku auth:token

faxxadf7-a340-434b-ad23-d2d51b4e7c1d
```

 Remember that we should never check this token into Git. It allows access to our entire Heroku account. Treat it with the same level of security as a password. We can, instead, store it in an environment variable and reference the variable in our code.

3. Now that our token is in `authentication.rb`, let's try running the file. If we added our token correctly, it will output a hash of our account information:

```
$ ruby authentication.rb

{"allow_tracking"=>true, "beta"=>false, "email"=>"coutermarsh.
mike@gmail.com", "id"=>"dxx1d923-35e1-4655-b333-f8b33db1e943",
"last_login"=>"2014-06-06T01:12:00Z", "name"=>nil, "two_factor_
authentication"=>false, "verified"=>true, "created_at"=>"2010-02-
03T03:34:45Z", "updated_at"=>"2014-08-09T19:40:35Z"}
```

4. When learning how to use a new gem, it can be useful to play around with its different functions in a Ruby console. This example project has a file set up for us to do this; this file is `console.rb`.

   Let's open `console.rb` and replace `your_token_here` with our authentication token, just like we did with `authentication.rb`.

5. Now that `console.rb` has our authentication token, let's run it. This time, it will bring up a Ruby console with an instance of the Platform API already instantiated and ready for us to use:

   ```
   $ ruby console.rb
   ```

6. For starters, let's try getting our account information from the console. This is exactly what `authentication.rb` did for us. We can do this by typing the following command in the console:

   ```
   $ heroku_api.account.info
   ```

   ```
   D, [2014-09-14T13:23:35.893920 #10391] DEBUG -- : [httplog]
   Sending: GET https://api.heroku.com:443/account
   D, [2014-09-14T13:23:35.894006 #10391] DEBUG -- : [httplog]
   Header: User-Agent: excon/0.39.5
   D, [2014-09-14T13:23:35.894046 #10391] DEBUG -- : [httplog]
   Header: Accept: application/vnd.heroku+json; version=3
   D, [2014-09-14T13:23:35.894087 #10391] DEBUG -- : [httplog]
   Header: Authorization: Bearer faf8adf9-a340-434b-ad23-d9d51b4e7c1d
   D, [2014-09-14T13:23:35.894136 #10391] DEBUG -- : [httplog]
   Header: Host: api.heroku.com:443
   D, [2014-09-14T13:23:36.180224 #10391] DEBUG -- : [httplog]
   Status: 200
   D, [2014-09-14T13:23:36.180752 #10391] DEBUG -- : [httplog]
   Benchmark: 0.286894 seconds
   => {"allow_tracking"=>true,
    "beta"=>false,
    "email"=>"coutermarsh.mike@gmail.com",
    "id"=>"dxx1d923-35e1-4655-b333-f8b33db1e943",
    "last_login"=>"2014-06-06T01:12:00Z",
    "name"=>nil,
    "two_factor_authentication"=>false,
    "verified"=>true,
    "created_at"=>"2010-02-03T03:34:45Z",
    "updated_at"=>"2014-08-09T19:40:35Z"}
   ```

7. In the output of the preceding command, take note of the [httplog] lines. These are shown because `console.rb` has `httplog` enabled. This is included in `console.rb` for learning purposes. It shows us the exact HTTP requests that the Platform API gem is making to the API.

   If we want to hide these, we can comment out the following lines in `console.rb`:

```
require 'httplog'
HttpLog.options[:log_response] = false
HttpLog.options[:log_headers] = true
HttpLog.options[:log_connect] = false
HttpLog.options[:logger] = Logger.new($stdout)
```

 The HTTPlog info will be omitted from the rest of the examples for readability.

8. This console uses Pry, which is a very powerful Ruby shell. We can use it to explore the Ruby code and the Platform API gem. If we want to see all of the possible methods available for an object, we can type `ls` and the object name. Let's run the following command to see the available methods on `account`:

```
$ ls -m heroku_api.account
```

```
PlatformAPI::Account#methods: change_email  change_password  info
update
```

 Pry's commands are based on Unix. The `ls` command is used to list, and `cd` is to navigate in and out of objects.

9. With Pry, we can quickly view the documentation for objects and methods with the `show-doc` command:

```
$ show-doc heroku_api.account
```

```
From: /Users/mcoutermarsh/.rvm/gems/ruby-2.1.2/gems/platform-
api-0.2.0/lib/platform-api/client.rb @ line 98:

Owner: PlatformAPI::Client

Visibility: public

Signature: account()

Number of lines: 3


An account represents an individual signed up to use the Heroku
platform.


return [Account]
```

10. If we'd like, we can even view all of the methods available for the entire Platform API gem with the following command:

```
$ ls -m heroku_api
```

11. We can also use show-doc to view method documentation. Let's try this now to learn about the change_password method:

```
$ show-doc heroku_api.account.change_password
```

```
From: /Users/mcoutermarsh/.rvm/gems/ruby-2.1.2/gems/platform-
api-0.2.0/lib/platform-api/client.rb @ line 377:

Owner: PlatformAPI::Account

Visibility: public

Signature: change_password(body)

Number of lines: 3


Change Password for account.


param body: the object to pass as the request payload
```

This lets us quickly see what the arguments for the change_password method are, without having to look up the documentation in a Web browser.

12. To finish up, we can close our console session by typing exit:

```
$ exit
```

How it works...

The Heroku Platform API gem takes care of the nitty-gritty details of making API requests for us, making it quick and easy to develop Ruby applications that make use of the Platform API. It knows exactly what endpoints to request and how to format each request. When using console.rb, we can learn about the exact endpoints that the gem is using by watching the httplog lines in the console. All of the parameters and headers are included in the log, thus showing the exact requests that are sent to the API.

Heroics

If we want to understand further how the Platform API gem was built, we can take a look at the Heroics gem. Heroics creates Ruby API wrappers based on a JSON schema of the API. Heroku used Heroics to create the Platform API gem.

 We can see the Platform API schema at https://github.com/heroku/platform-api/blob/master/lib/platform-api/schema.json.

Pry

In `console.rb`, we used Pry to set a break point in the execution of the file. This is a powerful skill to learn when building anything in Ruby. It makes debugging and exploring code much easier. Since the Platform API is well documented, we're able to use it to our advantage when getting familiar with it.

See also

▸ The Platform API gem at `https://github.com/heroku/platform-api`

▸ Pry at `http://pryrepl.org/`

▸ The Heroics Gem at `https://github.com/interagent/heroics`

▸ httplog at `https://github.com/trusche/httplog`

▸ Pry Byebug at `https://github.com/deivid-rodriguez/pry-byebug`

Scaling dynos and workers

Imagine if we could scale up our applications from our company chatroom? Or maybe even from our own custom admin panel? This is possible by integrating with the Heroku API. In this recipe, we'll be introduced to managing processes with the Platform API gem. This will give us the start we need to write our own code to handle scaling our Heroku applications.

 Be sure to complete the previous recipe before attempting this one.

How to do it...

Let's get started by opening up a terminal and navigating to our `heroku-api-examples` directory. Then, we can perform the following steps:

1. We can start by launching a console session to get familiar with the `app` commands:

   ```
   $ ruby console.rb
   ```

2. Now that we have a console session running, let's get a list of our available applications from the API using `app.list`. This will return an array of hashes. Each item in the array is one of our applications.

   We should set the response to a variable so that we can work with it later on.

   ```
   $ apps = heroku_api.app.list

     {"archived_at"=>nil,
      "buildpack_provided_description"=>"Ruby",
   ```

```
    "build_stack"=>{"id"=>"7e04461d-ec81-4bdd-8b37-b69b320a9f83",
"name"=>"cedar"},
    "created_at"=>"2014-04-20T22:32:57Z",
    "id"=>"7024121d-d91f-46a2-b008-78d637cff6fb",
    "git_url"=>"git@heroku.com:vote-a-tron.git",
    "maintenance"=>false,
    "name"=>"vote-a-tron",
    "owner"=>{"email"=>"coutermarsh.mike@gmail.com",
"id"=>"d3axx923-36e1-4655-b333-f8b33db1e943"},
    "region"=>{"id"=>"59accabd-516d-4f0e-83e6-6e3757701145",
"name"=>"us"},
    "released_at"=>"2014-06-21T21:23:13Z",
    "repo_size"=>802816,
    "slug_size"=>42519181,
    "stack"=>{"id"=>"7e04461d-ec81-4bdd-8b37-b69b320a9f83",
"name"=>"cedar"},
    "updated_at"=>"2014-06-21T21:23:13Z",
    "web_url"=>"http://vote-a-tron.herokuapp.com/"}]
```

3. The `apps` variable is now an array of all our applications. We can use it like we would use any array in Ruby. Let's look at a couple of examples of things we can do with this data.

    To see how many apps we have, we can use `count`:

    ```
    $ apps.count
    => 18
    ```

    To get an array of our all our app names, we can use `map`:

    ```
    $ apps.map{|app| app['name']}
    ```

    If we want to get information for only our Ruby apps, we can use `collect` with a regular expression match for Ruby:

    ```
    $ ruby_apps = apps.select{|app| /Ruby/ =~ app['buildpack_provided_
    description']}
    ```

     We use a regular expression here because the `buildpack` name might differ due to the framework used for each Ruby application.

4. If we want to get information for only a single application via the API, we can do this as well by specifying the application's name:

    ```
    $ heroku_api.app.info('app-name-here')
    ```

Remember that at any time, we can run `ls -m heroku_api.app` to see a list of the available methods for the `app` endpoint.

5. The specific processes that run for an application are available via the `formation` endpoint. Let's use this now to see the processes for one of our applications:

```
$ heroku_api.formation.list('app-name-here')
```

```
=> [{"command"=>"bundle exec rake jobs:work",
  "created_at"=>"2014-07-27T21:01:44Z",
  "id"=>"53a3f397-90a2-4e8c-a700-b5c4d1e27bb8",
  "type"=>"worker",
  "quantity"=>1,
  "size"=>"1X",
  "updated_at"=>"2014-07-27T21:01:44Z"},
 {"command"=>"bundle exec unicorn -p $PORT -c ./config/unicorn.
rb",
  "created_at"=>"2014-07-27T21:01:44Z",
  "id"=>"e1fd1c89-3876-4815-85b2-57dff996a375",
  "type"=>"web",
  "quantity"=>1,
  "size"=>"1X",
  "updated_at"=>"2014-07-27T21:01:44Z"},
 {"command"=>"bin/rails console",
  "created_at"=>"2014-07-27T21:01:44Z",
  "id"=>"f8c4b2e7-35e1-4adb-b806-f15abbcdfe12",
  "type"=>"console",
  "quantity"=>0,
  "size"=>"1X",
  "updated_at"=>"2014-07-27T21:01:44Z"},
 {"command"=>"bundle exec rake",
  "created_at"=>"2014-07-27T21:01:44Z",
  "id"=>"f291f5a8-853a-4131-ac28-3bf5423b8fac",
  "type"=>"rake",
  "quantity"=>0,
  "size"=>"1X",
  "updated_at"=>"2014-07-27T21:01:44Z"}]
```

6. If we want to limit this response to only a specific type of process, we can do that as well. Let's look at only `web` processes:

```
$ heroku_api.formation.info('app-name-here', 'web')
```

```
=> {"command"=>"bundle exec unicorn -p $PORT -c ./config/unicorn.
rb",
```

```
"created_at"=>"2014-07-27T21:01:44Z",
"id"=>"e1fd1c89-3876-4815-85b2-57dff996a375",
"type"=>"web",
"quantity"=>1,
"size"=>"1X",
"updated_at"=>"2014-07-27T21:01:44Z"}
```

7. Now, for the fun part, we can use `formation.update` to scale both the number and size of our processes. Let's start by scaling the number of web processes that we're running from 1 to 2:

```
$ heroku_api.formation.update('app-name-here', 'web', {quantity:
2})

=> {"command"=>"bundle exec unicorn -p $PORT -c ./config/unicorn.
rb",
"created_at"=>"2014-07-27T21:01:44Z",
"id"=>"e1fd1c89-3876-4815-85b2-57dff996a375",
"type"=>"web",
"quantity"=>2,
"size"=>"1X",
"updated_at"=>"2014-09-14T15:52:07Z"}
```

8. We can also scale the size of our processes. Let's try that now by bumping up our web process from a 1X dyno to a 2X dyno:

```
$ heroku_api.formation.update('app-name-here', 'web', {size:
'2X'})

=> {"command"=>"bundle exec unicorn -p $PORT -c ./config/unicorn.
rb",
"created_at"=>"2014-07-27T21:01:44Z",
"id"=>"e1fd1c89-3876-4815-85b2-57dff996a375",
"type"=>"web",
"quantity"=>2,
"size"=>"2X",
"updated_at"=>"2014-09-14T15:52:40Z"}
```

9. We can update both the size and quantity at once if we'd like:

```
$ heroku_api.formation.update('app-name-here', 'web', {quantity:
3, size: '2X'})
```

> Need more information on a specific command? Remember that with Pry, we can use the `show-doc` command to see documentation. Try it now with `show-doc heroku_api.formation.update`.

10. To finish up, let's not forget to scale our processes back to the original setting to avoid any unnecessary charges from Heroku:

```
$ heroku_api.formation.update('app-name-here', 'web', {quantity:
1, size: '1X'})
```

11. We can close our console session by typing `exit`:

```
$ exit
```

How it works...

In this recipe, we used the apps and formation API endpoints to view information about our application and its processes. The formation endpoint contains all the information about our application's different processes. With it, we're able to adjust the quantity or size of any process. We cannot create new process types from the API. This is only possible by making changes to our application's Procfile.

When using `console.rb` to test out the Platform API gem, remember that we can look at the output immediately after the command to see the HTTP requests made by the gem. If we were to use the API without the Ruby gem, these are the same requests we'd need to make to scale our applications.

See also

▶ For details on the app and formation endpoints, take a look at the Platform API documentation at `https://devcenter.heroku.com/articles/platform-api-reference`

Managing configuration variables

When enabling a Heroku add-on, such a Redis-to-go or MemCachier, the add-on automatically populates our configuration variables with the add-on credentials. They are able to do this because of the Heroku API. Configuration variables are a core part of any Heroku application. In this recipe, we'll learn how to manage them via the API.

 Be sure to read the *Getting started with the Platform API gem* recipe before attempting this recipe.

How to do it...

To begin, we can fire up a terminal and navigate to our `heroku-api-examples` directory. Then, we can perform the following steps:

1. We'll be practicing in the console. Let's start it up now:

    ```
    $ ruby console.rb
    ```

2. Let's take a look at the available commands for the config-vars endpoint by using Pry's `ls -m` command:

    ```
    $ ls -m heroku_api.config_var

    PlatformAPI::ConfigVar#methods: info  update
    ```

3. We can use the `info` command to view all of the configuration variables for an application. This command will return the variables in a hash:

    ```
    $ heroku_api.config_var.info('app-name')

    => {"RAILS_ENV"=>"production",
     "RACK_ENV"=>"production",
     "SECRET_KEY_BASE"=>"xxxy",
     "ADMIN_EMAILS"=>"coutermarsh.mike@gmail.com",
     "MEMCACHIER_SERVERS"=>"mc5.dev.ec2.memcachier.com:11211",
     "MEMCACHIER_PASSWORD"=>"xys",
     "MEMCACHIER_USERNAME"=>"abcd",

     "WEB_CONCURRENCY"=>"4"}
    ```

4. To update or create a configuration variable, we will use `update`:

    ```
    $ heroku_api.config_var.update('app-name', {test: 'testing')
    ```

    The command will return a hash with all of our configuration variables, including the one we just set.

 Remember that configuration variables are case sensitive.

5. We can update multiple values if we'd like:

    ```
    $ heroku_api.config_var.update('app-name', {test: 'testing';
    test2: 'another test')
    ```

6. To delete, we can pass `nil`:

    ```
    $ heroku_api.config_var.update('app-name', {test: nil})
    ```

7. To end our console session, we can type `exit`:

   ```
   $ exit
   ```

How it works...

In this recipe, we used the config-var API endpoint to make changes to our application's configuration variables.

Each change sent a request specifically to `https://api.heroku.com/apps/application-name/config-vars`.

If we watch the HTTP logs in the console, we can see what is happening beneath the surface for each request. To retrieve variables, a GET request is sent to the endpoint. To make changes or create existing variables, a PATCH request is used.

See also

▶ The config-vars documentation at `https://devcenter.heroku.com/articles/platform-api-reference#config-vars`

Adding and removing collaborators

When a new employee starts at our company, wouldn't it be great if we could quickly grant them access to all of our Heroku applications? We can write programs using the API to do this using the collaborator endpoint. In this recipe, we'll learn how to add and remove collaborators from our applications.

 Make sure you complete reading the *Getting Started with the Platform API gem* recipe before attempting this recipe.

How to do it...

To start, let's open a terminal and go to our `heroku-api-examples` directory. Then, we can perform the following steps:

1. Let's start up a console by running `console.rb`:

   ```
   $ ruby console.rb
   ```

2. With the collaborator's endpoint, we can list, create, or delete collaborators for any of our applications. Let's use the `list` command to see the current collaborators on one of our applications:

```
$ heroku_api.collaborator.list('app-name')

=> [{"created_at"=>"2014-04-20T22:32:57Z",
   "id"=>"059e7a76-ce3a-4e54-b655-54e3e8e2f253",
   "updated_at"=>"2014-04-20T22:32:57Z",
   "user"=>{"id"=>"d3a1d923-35e1-4655-b333-f8b33db1e943",
"email"=>"coutermarsh.mike@gmail.com"},
   "role"=>"owner"},
  {"created_at"=>"2014-06-06T02:31:25Z",
   "id"=>"7b803943-606f-4aa9-8021-bbb8aed04ba2",
   "updated_at"=>"2014-06-06T02:31:25Z",
   "user"=>{"id"=>"624252b3-960c-4dbf-b7bf-008d7e8310e6",
"email"=>"mike@mikecoutermarsh.com"}}]
```

3. To add a new collaborator to our application, we can use `create` and pass the user's e-mail address:

```
$ heroku_api.collaborator.create('app-name', {user: 'example@
example.com'})
```

4. When a user is invited, they'll be sent an e-mail that will notify them. We can optionally silence this e-mail invitation:

```
$ heroku_api.collaborator.create('app-name', {user: 'example@
example.com', silent: true})
```

5. Users can be removed with the `delete` command:

```
$ heroku_api.collaborator.delete('app-name', 'example@example.
com')
```

How it works...

We've now learned how to programmatically make use of the `collaborator` endpoint of the Heroku API. It will come in very useful when adding and removing users from our applications.

When deleting collaborators, there is one gotcha to be aware of. If the e-mail address has not yet signed up for a Heroku account, it will not be possible to remove them from the collaborator's list via the API. It will have do be done from either the dashboard or the CLI.

See also

▶ Take a look at the documentation on collaborators at `https://devcenter.heroku.com/articles/platform-api-reference#collaborator` for more information

Creating new Heroku applications

When starting a new Heroku application, it's pretty common that we'll find ourselves repeating the same steps. There is probably a set of add-ons that we find ourselves using over and over again. For a Rails app, we might find ourselves consistently setting up a stack with Postgres, MemCachier, LogEntries, and Rollbar. We can automate this!

In this recipe, you'll learn how to create applications and enable add-ons programmatically via the API.

 Be sure to read the *Getting started with the Platform API Gem* recipe before attempting this recipe.

How to do it...

Let's start by opening up a terminal and going to our `heroku-api-examples` directory. Then, we can perform the following steps:

1. We'll use Ruby in this recipe. Let's start it now by running `console.rb`:

   ```
   $ ruby console.rb
   ```

2. To create a new application, we can use `app.create`. We'll need to specify the application's name, its region (`us` or `eu`), and its Heroku stack. We should always use the latest stack, which at the time of writing this book is `cedar`:

   ```
   $ heroku_api.app.create({name: 'app-name', region: 'us', stack: 'cedar'})

   => {"archived_at"=>nil,
    "buildpack_provided_description"=>nil,
    "build_stack"=>{"id"=>"7e04461d-ec81-4bdd-8b37-b69b320a9f83",
   "name"=>"cedar"},
    "created_at"=>"2014-09-14T23:22:57Z",
    "id"=>"e1b241eb-9f83-4a07-8881-fef877144cc8",
    "git_url"=>"git@heroku.com:app-name.git",
    "maintenance"=>false,
    "name"=>"my-test-app1234",
   ```

```
"owner"=>{"email"=>"coutermarsh.mike@gmail.com", "id"=>"d3xxdx23-
35e1-4x55-b243-f8b33db1e943"},
  "region"=>{"id"=>"59accabd-516d-4f0e-83e6-6e3757701145",
"name"=>"us"},
  "released_at"=>"2014-09-14T23:22:57Z",
  "repo_size"=>nil,
  "slug_size"=>nil,
  "stack"=>{"id"=>"7e04461d-ec81-4bdd-8b37-b69b320a9f83",
"name"=>"cedar"},
  "updated_at"=>"2014-09-14T23:22:57Z",
  "web_url"=>"http://app-name.herokuapp.com/"}
```

3. Now that our application is created, we can start enabling add-ons for it. We can view our Heroku application's existing add-ons using `addon.list`. This will return a blank array since we just created the application:

```
heroku_api.addon.list('app-name')
=> []
```

4. Let's try adding the Heroku Postgres application. We can use `addon.create`. We need to pass our application's name to it, as well as a hash with the `plan` key set to the add-on we want enabled:

```
$ heroku_api.addon.create('app-name', {plan: 'heroku-
postgresql:dev'})
```

```
=> {"config_vars"=>["HEROKU_POSTGRESQL_CYAN_URL"],
  "created_at"=>"2014-09-14T23:30:55Z",
  "id"=>"0d1691e0-7c5c-4f95-b053-f22ac49bc7b2",
  "name"=>"heroku-postgresql-cyan",
  "addon_service"=>{"id"=>"6c67493d-8fc2-4cd4-9161-4f1ec11cbe69",
"name"=>"Heroku Postgres"},
  "plan"=>{"id"=>"95a1ce4c-c651-45dc-aaee-79b4603e76b7",
"name"=>"heroku-postgresql:dev"},
  "provider_id"=>"resource7869884@heroku.com",
  "updated_at"=>"2014-09-14T23:30:55Z"}
```

5. Next, let's add MemCachier:

```
$ heroku_api.addon.create('app-name', {plan: 'memcachier'})
```

```
=> {"config_vars"=>["MEMCACHIER_SERVERS", "MEMCACHIER_USERNAME",
"MEMCACHIER_PASSWORD"],
  "created_at"=>"2014-09-14T23:34:12Z",
  "name"=>"memcachier",
  "addon_service"=>{"id"=>"92d8bf99-50ce-4889-af22-78518d503dd3",
"name"=>"MemCachier"},
```

```
"plan"=>{"id"=>"ec8d756b-6995-4890-8589-bdc8afa098bc",
"name"=>"memcachier:dev"},

"provider_id"=>"47536",

"id"=>"c5dde380-7877-4663-9a62-c54f7d43b3f6",

"updated_at"=>"2014-09-14T23:34:12Z"}
```

 We can get the plan name for any add-on by going to https://addons.heroku.com and selecting an add-on. At the bottom of the page, the CLI command to enable the add-on is shown. The plan is the last argument, for example, heroku addons:add memcachier.

How it works...

We just programmatically created a Heroku application from Ruby using the API. Unfortunately, we cannot push code to an application via the API. We'll still have to do this from Git.

Heroku has a solution to deploy open source applications from outside the CLI. It's called Heroku Button. It sets up an application in a manner similar to what we did here, with the addition of making the initial code push from an open source repository.

See also

▶ Learn about Heroku Button at https://devcenter.heroku.com/articles/heroku-button

▶ App documentation available at https://devcenter.heroku.com/articles/platform-api-reference#app

▶ Add-on documentation available at https://devcenter.heroku.com/articles/platform-api-reference#add-on

Index

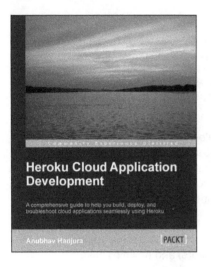

Heroku Cloud Application Development

ISBN: 978-1-78355-097-5   Paperback: 336 pages

A comprehensive guide to help you build, deploy, and troubleshoot cloud applications seamlessly using Heroku

1. Understand the concepts of the Heroku platform: how it works, the application development stack, and security features.

2. Learn how to build, deploy, and troubleshoot a cloud application in the most popular programming languages easily and quickly using Heroku.

3. Leverage the book's practical examples to build your own "real" Heroku cloud applications in no time.

Force.com Development Blueprints

ISBN: 978-1-78217-245-1   Paperback: 350 pages

Design and develop real-world, cutting-edge cloud applications using the powerful Force.com development framework

1. Create advanced cloud applications using the best Force.com technologies.

2. Bring your cloud application ideas to market faster using the proven Force.com infrastructure.

3. Step-by-step tutorials show you how to quickly develop real-world cloud applications.

Please check **www.PacktPub.com** for information on our titles

Learning Play! Framework 2

ISBN: 978-1-78216-012-0   Paperback: 290 pages

Start developing awesome web applications with this friendly, practical guide to the Play! Framework

1. While driving in Java, tasks are also presented in Scala—a great way to be introduced to this amazing language.

2. Create a fully-fledged, collaborative web application—starting from ground zero; all layers are presented in a pragmatic way.

3. Gain the advantages associated with developing a fully integrated web framework.

SproutCore Web Application Development

ISBN: 978-1-84951-770-6   Paperback: 194 pages

Creating fast, powerful, and feature-rich web applications using the SproutCore HTML5 framework

1. Write next-gen HTML5 apps using the SproutCore framework and tools.

2. Get started right away by creating a powerful application in the very first chapter.

3. Build your understanding of SproutCore as you follow through the most complete reference to the framework anywhere in existence.

Please check **www.PacktPub.com** for information on our titles